VOLUME TWO

Women in Islam

GLIMPSES OF TRUE BEAUTY FROM THE LIVES OF PIOUS WOMEN

PUBLISHED BY:
ISLAMIC BOOK STORE

Glimpses of
True Beauty
from the Lives of
Pious Women

Volume 2

A humble appeal is made to the readers to offer suggestions, corrections, etc. to improve the quality of this publication in the future. May Allah Ta'ala reward you for this.

The writers, editors and typesetters humbly request your du'aas for them, their parents, families, Asaatizah and Mashaayikh.

Prepared By:

Uswatul Muslimah

4 Third Avenue
P.O. Box 26024
Isipingo Beach
4115
South Africa

Tel: +27 31 902 9818 (ext. 6)

WhatsApp: +27 72 566 4856

First Edition: Zul Hijjah 1441 / August 2020

Published By:
302 Saad Residancy
Sahin Park
M G Road Bardoli
394601
India

True beauty is the beauty which resides within the heart.

Contents

Introduction 1

Before Islam 5

    Safety and Security in Chastity 7

    Allah is Sufficient 11

    Wife of Nabi Ayyoob ('alaihis salaam) 14

        Through Thick and Thin 14

        Faithfulness is Never Forgotten 16

    Begging for the Best 21

    Sayyidah Maryam ('alaihas salaam) 24

        The Best of Women 24

        Dedicated for Deen 25

        Raised in Righteousness 28

        The 'Produce' of Piety 30

        The Preparation of Piety 33

        Pleased with His Decree 35

        Maintaining Modesty 36

        The Recipe to Raise Pious Offspring 38

    Loyal to the Last 41

    The Fruit of Charity and Fire of Jealousy 46

    Sustained from His Unseen Treasures 51

Era of the Sahaabah (radhiyallahu 'anhum) 55

   First Impressions 57

   "Are You Blind?" 60

   Sayyidah 'Aaishah (radhiyallahu 'anha) 62

      The Most Beloved of the Most Beloved 62

      Spontaneous Modesty 64

      Sublime Display of Submission 67

      The Resource that Remains 70

      Eat to Live, Not Live to Eat 72

      Forgiven and Forgotten 75

      Firm Faith in Allah 77

      Passion for Spending on the Poor 79

      Selfless Consideration 83

      Humble to the Last 86

   Sayyidah Safiyyah (radhiyallahu 'anha) 89

      Slavery over Freedom 89

      Exemplary Respect 91

      Loyal to Islam 93

   Unquestioning Submission 96

   Allah before Emotions 101

   Modesty – No Matter What! 104

The Supportive Spouse 106

Glimpses of True Love 109

Absolute Submission 114

Sayyidah Asmaa bintu 'Umais (radhiyallahu 'anha) 117

    Blessed with the Best 117

    Competing in Kindness and Care 119

    Happiness in Deeni Progress 123

    Bidding her Husband Farewell 126

    The First Covered Bier in Islam 131

    The Faithful Wife 133

    Steadfast in Adversity 135

Early Centuries of Islam 137

    Piety in Public and in Privacy 139

    Righteousness is Always Rewarded 143

    A Partner to Paradise 147

    Ummul Baneen (rahimahallah) 150

        Piety in the Palace 150

        Passion to Spend in the Path of Allah 153

        The Priority of Purity 156

        Worried for the Welfare of Others 158

        Sorrow for her Statement 161

Zubaidah (rahimahallah) (rahimahallah) 164

    Leaving a Legacy 164

    The Passion to Share 165

    Determined to Make a Difference 168

    At the Forefront of Relief Efforts 172

    Respecting the Symbols of Islam 176

Cautious in Consumption 179

The Gleaming Jewel 183

Grateful before the Giver 186

Uninfluenced by Others 189

Latter Centuries of Islam 191

Wife of Moulana Qaasim Naanotwi (rahimahullah) 193

    The Silent and Unseen Pillar 193

    Taking out Time 194

    From Luxury to Simplicity 196

    A Submissive Spouse 199

    Going the Extra Mile 201

Mother of Moulana 'Umar Paalanpuri (rahimahullah) 204

    Moulded by His Mother 204

    Shaping the Mindset 206

    Instilling Qualities of Imaan 209

Making Her Dream a Reality 211

The Fruit of Her Effort 214

Mother of Moulana Abul Hasan 'Ali Nadwi (rahimahullah) 218

An Exemplary Mother 218

The Environment of Righteousness 220

Carefully Controlled Education 223

The First Haafizah 225

A Husband of Deen or Dunya? 228

Making the Marriage 231

Going Above and Beyond 233

Dealing with the Demise of Her Husband 235

Committed to Du'aa and 'Ibaadah 237

An Upbringing of Piety 240

Dedicating her Son for Deen 242

An Envious End 244

Index 249

Introduction

Throughout history, people have inhabited different regions of the world, spoken different languages, experienced different cultures and witnessed different spectacles. However, all people, from all places and times, eventually and ultimately arrived at the same conclusion – physical beauty is only skin deep, while true beauty resides within the heart of an individual.

The French have a proverb that states, "Beauty without virtue is like a flower without fragrance." Likewise, the Burmese say, "Good character is the true beauty that never fades." Similarly, the Chinese have a saying, "If there is light in the soul, there will be beauty in the person."

All these proverbs are diverse in their origins but concur on the same point – true beauty lies in cultivating good character and praiseworthy traits.

As Muslims, our leader in life, and in the afterlife, is Rasulullah (sallallahu 'alaihi wasallam) – the pinnacle of perfection from all of Allah Ta'ala's creation who was the very embodiment of both inner and outer beauty. Through following his guidance and his blessed way, we will be able to imbibe those values and qualities that will bring true beauty to our hearts and souls.

One cannot choose the features and appearance that he was given by birth. If one finds his nose too round, or ears too large, or lips too thin, then normally, there is nothing much that he can do to alter or improve it. However, as far as inner beauty goes, not even the sky is the limit. One can develop such inner beauty that the eyes of the heart will be dazzled. Furthermore, while physical beauty has a 'best before' date, as it naturally fades with the progression of age, the beauty of the soul only continues increasing and is only enhanced with time.

In a day and age where society obsesses over every minute aspect of external beauty, the quest for internal beauty is often overlooked and neglected – whereas it is one's internal beauty that fetches value in the sight of Allah Ta'ala. Hence, Rasulullah (sallallahu 'alaihi wasallam) once mentioned, "Indeed Allah Ta'ala does not look at your appearances (i.e. your external beauty) and wealth, rather He looks at your hearts (i.e. your inner beauty) and your actions." *(Saheeh Muslim #6543)*

In the quest to develop inner beauty, inspirational incidents from the lives of others treading the path of piety prove very beneficial and motivational. Often, when one has hit a rock-bottom low, and has stumbled and fallen so many times that he has lost the courage to wake up once again, it is these stories that give us a glimmer of hope and shine a ray of inspiration in our darkest moments.

This book is the second volume in the True Beauty series, and has also been compiled from the stories of pious women posted on the Uswatul Muslimah website. Studying the incidents of these personalities and pondering over the lessons learnt from their lives will assist us to reflect over our own lives and inspire us to acquire the TRUE BEAUTY with which they had been blessed.

May Allah Ta'ala accept this effort, allow us to follow in the footsteps of these saintly souls and raise us with them on the Day of Qiyaamah, aameen.

Before Islam

Safety and Security in Chastity

On one occasion, Nabi Ebrahim ('alaihis salaam) was travelling through Egypt with his respected wife, Sayyidah Saarah ('alaihas salaam), when they were apprehended by the men of the evil and tyrant king of Egypt. The king had received news of the immense beauty of Sayyidah Saarah ('alaihas salaam) and had thus sent his men to abduct her.

When Sayyidah Saarah ('alaihas salaam) was taken away, Nabi Ebrahim ('alaihis salaam) began to earnestly engage in salaah and du'aa. Allah Ta'ala raised the veil of the unseen, allowing him to observe the events transpiring between Sayyidah Saarah ('alaihas salaam) and the king.

When Sayyidah Saarah ('alaihas salaam) reached the king, and he wished to make evil advances towards her, she made wudhu and engaged in salaah. She made du'aa saying, "O Allah! You are fully aware that I have brought imaan in You and Your Rasul (Nabi Ebrahim ['alaihis salaam])! I have safeguarded my chastity (and reserved myself) for my husband alone, so do not allow this disbeliever to have any power over me!"

This du'aa of Sayyidah Saarah ('alaihas salaam) was instantly answered and drew the immediate assistance of Allah Ta'ala. Hence, as the king advanced towards her, he was struck with sudden paralysis, choked and fell to the ground. The tyrant begged Sayyidah Saarah ('alaihas salaam) to make du'aa for his health to be restored, promising to release her if she did so. Since the king had promised to release her, and she feared that the people would accuse her of killing the king, Sayyidah Saarah ('alaihas salaam) made du'aa for his health to be restored.

Allah Ta'ala accepted her du'aa and the king recovered. However, he once again made evil advances towards her. Sayyidah Saarah ('alaihas salaam) once again resorted to salaah and du'aa, causing the king to collapse for the second time. Thereafter, due to his pleading and promise to release her, she made du'aa again and his health was restored.

The king was so persistent in advancing towards Sayyidah Saarah ('alaihas salaam) that he again made advances towards her! Finally, after being struck with paralysis for a third or fourth time and regaining his health, he said to his people, "You did not bring a human being to me! You have actually brought a devil!"

The king then addressed Sayyidah Saarah ('alaihas salaam) saying, "O lady! (How is it that) your Rabb was so loyal to you when you supplicated to Him against me." She replied, "If you are obedient to Him, He will be loyal to you as well."

He then allowed her to go and gifted her with a slave girl, named Haajar, as a servant.

(Saheeh Bukhaari #3358, Musnad Ahmad #9241, Fat-hul Baari, Al-Bidaayah wan Nihaayah vol. 1, pg. 183 and Taareekh Ibni 'Asaakir vol. 69, pg. 185)

Lessons:

🌸 The solution to all our problems is in resorting to salaah and du'aa. When beset by this great test, Sayyidah Saarah ('alaihas salaam) and Nabi Ebrahim ('alaihis salaam) both stood in salaah, seeking the help of Allah Ta'ala. If we face any problem, we should turn to Allah Ta'ala first. We should make wudhu, perform salaah and make du'aa, begging Him for assistance.

🌸 When Sayyidah Saarah ('alaihas salaam) had turned to Allah Ta'ala in her hour of need, she presented two deeds before Him in order to attract His divine help and assistance. The first deed that Sayyidah Saarah ('alaihas salaam) presented was her imaan and the second was her chastity. Mentioning her chastity in this crucial situation is a clear proof that she was absolutely confident and certain of herself in this regard, and this apparently became the means of drawing the immediate help of Allah Ta'ala. In fact, there are numerous incidents of people who enjoyed the special assistance of Allah Ta'ala due to safeguarding their chastity.

🌸 Sayyidah Saarah ('alaihas salaam) highlighted the principle of Allah Ta'ala – if a person is loyal to Him, Allah Ta'ala will be loyal to him as well. If he is obedient to Allah Ta'ala in times of prosperity, Allah Ta'ala will be there for him in times of adversity. In essence, Allah Ta'ala will readily answer his du'aas. Very often, it happens that when a person is undergoing some difficulty, he sincerely turns to Allah Ta'ala in desperation, making all types of pledges and promises. However, no sooner is the difficulty alleviated, then he reverts to his evil ways and forgets Allah Ta'ala. This is not true loyalty but is rather a convenience relationship which will not secure the goodness that a person is desirous of.

❁   The abundant rewards for the one who makes an effort to protect his chastity are not restricted to the Hereafter. Rather, its fruits are enjoyed in this very world as well. Hence, Sayyidah Saarah ('alaihas salaam) was rewarded immediately, in this very world, with a slave girl to serve her and attend to her needs.

Allah is Sufficient

When Nabi Ebrahim ('alaihis salaam) left his wife, Sayyidah Haajar ('alaihas salaam), with her infant child, Nabi Ismaa'eel ('alaihis salaam), in the barren land of Makkah Mukarramah, as per the command of Allah Ta'ala, Sayyidah Haajar ('alaihas salaam) asked him, "O Ebrahim! Where are you going, leaving us in this valley wherein we have no companion or anything else?" Her question was however, met with silence from Nabi Ebrahim ('alaihis salaam).

Sayyidah Haajar ('alaihas salaam) repeated the question, but to no avail. She finally rephrased the question and asked, "Has Allah Ta'ala commanded you to do this?" When Nabi Ebrahim ('alaihis salaam) replied in the affirmative, she exclaimed, "In that case, He will not allow us to perish. I am pleased with (the command of) Allah Ta'ala. He is sufficient for me."

After some time, the meagre provisions that she had with her depleted. She was thus overcome by thirst, as a result of which her milk dried and she was unable to suckle her son. Nabi Ismaa'eel ('alaihis salaam) became thirsty to such an extent that he began rolling in the sand while kicking his heels on the ground, and he even began to experience difficulty in breathing! Unable to bear this sight, Sayyidah Haajar ('alaihas salaam) commenced running between two nearby mountains, Safaa and Marwah, earnestly seeking someone to help her.

On the seventh round, whilst on Marwah, Sayyidah Haajar ('alaihas salaam) heard a sound. As she looked towards the sound, she suddenly saw Jibreel ('alaihis salaam) standing at the place that thereafter became the well of Zam-zam.

Jibreel ('alaihis salaam) asked Sayyidah Haajar ('alaihas salaam), "Who are you?" She replied, "I am Haajar, the mother of the child of Ebrahim ('alaihis salaam)." Jibreel ('alaihis salaam) then enquired from her, "To whom has your husband entrusted you?" She answered, "To Allah!" Jibreel ('alaihis salaam) declared, "He has entrusted you to that Being Who will suffice your every need."

(Saheeh Bukhaari #3364 and Fat-hul Baari)

Lessons:

❁ No amount of human intelligence could have fathomed the wisdom behind this command of Allah Ta'ala to Nabi Ebrahim ('alaihis salaam), as abandoning a woman and an infant child in a desert without any apparent means of survival outwardly seems foolish. However, Sayyidah Haajar ('alaihas salaam) displayed the true spirit of submission. As soon as she came to know that it was on Allah Ta'ala's command that she was being left in that barren land, she expressed complete submission. She did not respond with 'buts' by saying, "But what if?", "But I can't understand this!", "But it doesn't make sense!", or "But I can't manage this!" Rather, her response is worthy of being engraved in gold and etched onto the heart of every believer.

❀   Sometimes the thought might cross the mind of being unable to manage life's challenges or to practise on Deen in today's environment. Sayyidah Haajar ('alaihas salaam) gave the answer thousands of years ago, when she was staring at her destruction – Allah Ta'ala will never place a servant in a situation that is unbearable. He will never neglect the one who follows His commands. The command of Allah Ta'ala and the way of His messenger as a rule is never beyond a person's ability. All it requires is a bit of courage in the beginning. Then the road opens up.

❀   When our gaze is constantly fixed on Allah Ta'ala and we have deep conviction in Him, we will be prepared to make every sacrifice for His sake and we will not become victims of depression and despondency even in the most challenging of situations. Allah Ta'ala is the only Being that can be sufficient for a person. Hence, a person needs to place his complete trust and reliance on Allah Ta'ala, and He will take care of him and be sufficient for him.

Wife of Nabi Ayyoob ('alaihis salaam)

Through Thick and Thin

The incident of Nabi Ayyoob ('alaihis salaam) is well known to one and all. Initially, Nabi Ayyoob ('alaihis salaam) enjoyed great prosperity. He had an abundance of animals and crops, many children and numerous homes. Allah Ta'ala then decided to test him. He lost all his wealth, all his children and was afflicted with a disease which ravaged his entire body. The only two limbs of his body that were spared from this illness were his tongue and his heart. Despite these adversities, even in this condition, he would keep his heart and tongue engaged in the remembrance of Allah Ta'ala.

While Nabi Ayyoob ('alaihis salaam) patiently endured this test, most of the people abandoned him, until he was left alone and isolated in a corner of the town. Only his loyal wife did not desert or abandon him. According to some historians, her name was Layyaa, while others have mentioned that her name was Rahmah.

She remembered his favours upon her when conditions were favourable and prosperous, and remained at his side through thick and thin, ever loyal and faithful.

She would patiently tend to him and saw to all his needs. In some narrations, it has even been mentioned that when her wealth was eventually depleted, she undertook domestic work in peoples' homes to earn a living so that she could continue to see to her ailing husband's needs. This was apart from her losing all her children. Through all these tests, however, she remained patient and did not complain, even though she went from a life of comfort and happiness to one of difficulty and distress.

(Al-Bidaayah wan Nihaayah vol. 1, pg. 262)

Lessons:

The proverb "a friend in need is a friend indeed" is often quoted, highlighting the fact that a true friend is one who will remain with you in difficult times as well as good times. We can imagine that if such loyalty is expected of a good friend, then what must be the high level of loyalty that is expected of a true spouse? After all, the relationship between a husband and wife far surpasses any friendship! Hence, a true and loyal wife is not one who will abscond to her father's house when "the going gets tough". Rather, she will patiently remain with her husband and assist him, to the best of her ability, as she would expect of him had she been in difficulty.

❀   Undergoing tests is an unavoidable occurrence in life. We cannot choose the nature or time of our tests – but we can choose to pass the tests. To do so, we will have to hold firmly to sabr (patience) and remain pleased with the decision of Allah Ta'ala.

Faithfulness is Never Forgotten

Nabi Ayyoob ('alaihis salaam) remained in a state of illness for more than eighteen years, yet he and his respected wife remained patient and steadfast.

One day, Shaitaan approached the wife of Nabi Ayyoob ('alaihis salaam) in the guise of a doctor. As he had adopted this form and appeared to be a 'normal' person, she did not realize that it was actually Shaitaan standing in front of her. Thinking him to be a doctor, out of concern for her husband, she asked him for a cure for her husband's illness. Shaitaan replied, "I do have a cure. However, in return for the cure, he must address me and say, 'You have cured me'. I do not want any other compensation for my treatment."

Nabi Ayyoob's ('alaihis salaam) wife returned to him and informed him of what had transpired. As soon as he heard this, he realized that the 'man' was no doctor, but was none other than

Shaitaan. Being the Nabi of Allah Ta'ala, Nabi Ayyoob ('alaihis salaam) was angered that his wife would even suggest that he utter such words, attributing the cure to Shaitaan. Hence, Nabi Ayyoob ('alaihis salaam) vowed to lash his wife one hundred times.

This incident greatly grieved Nabi Ayyoob ('alaihis salaam), as Shaitaan was now trying to mislead his wife. Nabi Ayyoob ('alaihis salaam) thus made du'aa to Allah Ta'ala, asking Allah Ta'ala to cure him, saying, "Indeed Shaitaan has afflicted me with distress and suffering." Allah Ta'ala accepted his du'aa and instructed him in the following words, "Strike with your foot, here is (water for) a cool bath and to drink".

As he did so, a spring of water gushed forth. Nabi Ayyoob ('alaihis salaam) then drank the water and bathed in it. Allah Ta'ala placed the cure for his illness in this water, and through drinking it and bathing in it, he was completely cured of his illness.

Thereafter, Allah Ta'ala sent him a garment of Jannah. When his wife arrived to tend to him, according to her routine, she failed to find him. Instead, she saw a man seated nearby and asked him, "Have you seen the ill-man who used to be here?" She was griefstricken and feared that perhaps he had been killed by wild animals. The man replied that he was actually Nabi Ayyoob ('alaihis salaam). Initially, she was hesitant to believe him, but he then told her how Allah Ta'ala had cured him of his illness.

Allah Ta'ala then restored her youth and allowed her to bear Nabi Ayyoob ('alaihis salaam) children once again. According to some reports, she gave birth to twenty-six sons, while other reports mention that Allah Ta'ala even brought all their deceased children back to life. Allah Ta'ala also sent two clouds to him; the first filled one threshing floor of his with gold, while the second cloud filled his other threshing floor with silver. In this manner, Allah Ta'ala replaced everything that he had lost and granted him even more than he initially had.

Nabi Ayyoob ('alaihis salaam) now needed to fulfil his vow. Allah Ta'ala told Nabi Ayyoob ('alaihis salaam) that instead of lashing her one hundred times, he should take a bundle containing one hundred pieces of straw, and lash her once with it. In this manner, the vow will be fulfilled. Allah Ta'ala says, "And take in your hand a bunch of grass and strike with it, and do not break your oath."

Allah Ta'ala instructed Nabi Ayyoob ('alaihis salaam) to fulfil his vow in this manner as Allah Ta'ala valued her loyalty, faithfulness and obedience to her husband, as well as the patience and obedience of Nabi Ayyoob ('alaihis salaam). Therefore, Allah Ta'ala mentions immediately thereafter, "Indeed, We found him patient. What an excellent servant! Indeed, he always turned to Allah."

(Surah Saad, v41-44, Al-Bidaayah wan Nihaayah vol. 1, pgs. 262-266 and Majma'uz Zawaaid #13821)

Lessons:

❀ Many people have good intentions and praiseworthy motives. They sincerely wish to assist people and bring about their betterment. However, together with the intention being correct, it is necessary that the means adopted should also be pleasing to Allah Ta'ala.

❀ The Ambiyaa ('alaihimus salaam) were such that their happiness and their displeasure were purely for the sake of Allah Ta'ala. In other words, if they suffered any personal grievance, they would overlook and forgive. However, if the law of Allah Ta'ala was broken, they would become angry, for the sake of Allah Ta'ala, and act in accordance with the command of Allah Ta'ala. Similarly, the Ambiyaa ('alaihmus salaam) would only express happiness if the occasion was one which Allah Ta'ala approved of. Hence, the challenge is for us to similarly make our pleasure and displeasure subject to the pleasure and displeasure of Allah Ta'ala. Therefore, if our children do not perform their salaah, it should anger us and prompt us to discipline them. However, if they accidentally break some item of ours, we should overlook and forgive them.

❀ Allah Ta'ala never forgets the loyalty of His servants. Hence, whether in this world or the next, He will most certainly acknowledge their efforts and reward them. Thus, due to her patience, perseverance and loyalty, Allah Ta'ala Himself told Nabi Ayyoob ('alaihis salaam) of a method through which his wife would be saved from the hundred lashes. Similarly, if we remain loyal to Allah Ta'ala, He will be there for us in our time of need.

   As severe as the sickness of Nabi Ayyoob ('alaihis salaam) was, he bore it patiently and did not become greatly worried or perturbed. However, when Shaitaan attempted to misguide his wife, he became extremely worried and turned to Allah Ta'ala in du'aa. Hence, we understand that one of the greatest worries and concerns that we should have is for the guidance and piety of our families. We should constantly make du'aa for this and encourage them towards righteousness.

Begging for the Best

On one occasion, Rasulullah (sallallahu 'alaihi wasallam) visited a bedouin who received him warmly and honoured him. So, Rasulullah (sallallahu 'alaihi wasallam) reciprocated and bade the bedouin to also visit him.

When the bedouin arrived, Rasulullah (sallallahu 'alaihi wasallam) said to him, "If you have any need, you may ask me." The bedouin replied, "I want a she-camel to use as a conveyance, and a few goats for my family to milk."

On hearing his reply, Rasulullah (sallallahu 'alaihi wasallam) addressed the Sahaabah (radhiyallahu 'anhum) and said, "Why do you not be like the old woman of the Banu Israaeel?" The Sahaabah (radhiyallahu 'anhum) asked, "O Rasul of Allah (sallallahu 'alaihi wasallam)! Who was the old woman of the Banu Israaeel and what was her incident?"

Rasulullah (sallallahu 'alaihi wasallam) replied by relating the following incident:

When Nabi Moosa ('alaihis salaam) departed from Egypt with the Banu Israaeel, they could not find the road (which they needed to travel on). So Nabi Moosa ('alaihis salaam) asked the Banu Israaeel, "What is the matter (i.e. why is it that we cannot find the road)?" The learned among the Banu Israaeel answered, "When Yusuf ('alaihis salaam) was close to passing away, he made us pledge in the name of Allah Ta'ala that we will not leave Egypt, without taking his body with us." Nabi Moosa ('alaihis salaam) then asked, "Who knows the location of the grave of Yusuf ('alaihis salaam)?" They replied that an old woman knew the location. Nabi Moosa ('alaihis salaam) thus sent for her.

When she arrived, Nabi Moosa ('alaihis salaam) requested, "Guide me to the grave of Yusuf ('alaihis salaam)." However, the old woman responded, "(I will not do so) until you give me what I want." Nabi Moosa ('alaihis salaam) asked her, "What is it that you want?" She replied, "I want to be with you in Jannah." Initially, Nabi Moosa ('alaihis salaam) was reluctant to accede to her request, but Allah Ta'ala sent revelation to him, commanding him to agree to the old woman's request.

She then proceeded with them to a lake and instructed them to drain all its water. When this was completed, she instructed them to dig until they discovered the grave of Nabi Yusuf ('alaihis salaam).

Once they recovered the body, removed it from the grave and carried it with them, the road became as clear as daylight for them.

(Saheeh Ibni Hibbaan #723)

Lesson:

❀ Imagine that it was Lailatul Qadr (the Night of Power), or you managed to cling to the Ka'bah at the multazam, and you now had a 'once in a lifetime chance' to make a du'aa that you greatly hope will gain acceptance. What would you ask for? Perhaps many of us would ask for something related to this world such as beauty, health, wealth, a dream home, etc.

However, Rasulullah (sallallahu 'alaihi wasallam) praised the old woman of the Banu Israaeel and encouraged the Sahaabah (radhiyallahu 'anhum) to be like her. When she saw the golden opportunity, instead of asking for something paltry and insignificant, she seized her chance to secure Jannah for herself.

Thus, when the hadeeth teaches us to make du'aa for all our needs, whether big or small, we should not suffice on asking only for our small needs while neglecting to ask for Jannah. Instead, we must make it a priority to beg for Jannah, as this is the biggest need.

Sayyidah Maryam ('alaihas salaam)

The Best of Women

Sayyidah Maryam ('alaihas salaam) was a woman especially honoured by Allah Ta'ala in a unique manner – an entire surah of the Quraan Majeed is named after her. She is also the only woman whose name is mentioned, not once, but repeatedly in the Quraan Majeed.

In Surah Aal 'Imraan (v42), Allah Ta'ala mentions how He instructed the angels to announce to Sayyidah Maryam ('alaihas salaam), "O Maryam! Indeed Allah Ta'ala has selected you, purified you and chosen you above all women."

Rasulullah (sallallahu 'alaihi wasallam) similarly attested to the great virtue of Sayyidah Maryam ('alaihas salaam). He (sallallahu 'alaihi wasallam) mentioned, "Khadeejah (radhiyallahu 'anha) is superior in virtue to all the women of my Ummah, just as Maryam ('alaihas salaam) was superior in virtue to all the women of the previous eras." *(Tabraani and Bazzaar - Majma'uz Zawaaid #15260)*

The life of Sayyidah Maryam ('alaihas salaam) was unique and has many important and beneficial lessons to teach us. In studying her life, we can identify the outstanding qualities and attributes which Allah Ta'ala had blessed her with, and for which He and Rasulullah (sallallahu 'alaihi wasallam) praised her in such glowing words. We should therefore strive to inculcate them in our lives so that we too may gain the acceptance of Allah Ta'ala.

Dedicated for Deen

The mother and father of Sayyidah Maryam ('alaihas salaam) were 'Imraan and Hannah. Before the birth of Sayyidah Maryam ('alaihas salaam), Hannah was unable to bear a child.

One day, Hannah observed a bird feeding its chick. Seeing this spectacle of love and compassion, her heart was overcome by the desire to have a child. She thus turned to Allah Ta'ala in du'aa, begging him to bless her with a child. Her du'aa was answered and soon thereafter she conceived. She vowed to Allah Ta'ala that she would dedicate her child to worshipping Him and serving Masjidul Aqsa. *(Surah Aal 'Imraan v35 and Tafseer Ibni Katheer vol. 2, pg. 337)*

When the child was born, Hannah noticed that it was a girl! Normally only a male child would be dedicated for serving in the masjid and worshipping Allah Ta'ala. Nevertheless, Hannah understood that Allah Ta'ala knew best, and it was in His infinite wisdom that He had blessed her with a daughter, instead of a son. *(Surah Aal 'Imraan v36, Tafseerul Qurtubi vol. 5, pg. 101 and Tafseerul Madaarik vol. 1, pg. 172)*

Hannah named her daughter 'Maryam' which meant 'worshipper' in the language of the time. Her intention was that depite her baby being a female and thus not being able to serve in the masjid, she will still dedicate her to worshipping Allah Ta'ala. *(Surah Aal 'Imraan v36, Tafseerul Madaarik vol. 1, pg. 173 and Bayaanul Quraan vol. 1, pg. 222)*

Hannah then made a special du'aa saying, "I seek Your protection (O Allah) for her and her progeny from Shaitaan the rejected."

Whenever a child is born, Shaitaan interferes with the child and pokes it, causing it to cry out aloud. However, through the blessing of this du'aa of Hannah, Sayyidah Maryam ('alaihas salaam) and her son, Nabi 'Isa ('alaihis salaam), were both safeguarded from Shaitaan and thus did not cry when they were born. *(Surah Aal 'Imraan v36 and Saheeh Bukhaari #3286 & #4548)*

Lessons:

🌹 Every person has unfulfilled wishes, desires and aspirations. Regardless of what the desire may be, the only One Who can fulfill our ambition is Allah Ta'ala. Hence, even though we adopt the means, we believe, from our hearts, that only Allah

Ta'ala can make the means effective. After all, there are so many people who undergo fertility treatments, yet still fail to conceive.

❀ The ambition of Hannah was not merely to have a child, but rather to dedicate her child to the worship of Allah Ta'ala and to serving the masjid. There are many parents who, even before the birth of their children, plan their career path, whether in medicine, law, engineering, etc. However, how many parents plan for their children to be the worshippers of Allah Ta'ala and their sons to be devotees of the masjid? How many parents take steps to ensure that their children attend the best madrasahs and acquire the best Deeni upbringing and education? These are the ultimate 'careers' as these 'professions' bear profits in the Hereafter.

❀ We all plan and hope for our lives to work out in a certain way. However, Allah Ta'ala knows what is best for us and blesses us accordingly. We should always be happy and content with the decree of Allah Ta'ala and should be appreciative of His favour upon us, as we do not even deserve any of His bounties.

❀ When her child was born, the concern of Hannah was for her child to be protected from Shaitaan. Hence, every parent, from before their child is even born, should worry about the safety of their child's imaan and take the appropriate steps to safeguard their Deen. Together with putting the necessary measures in place, we have to make constant du'aa to Allah Ta'ala to safeguard them from all evil and sin.

Raised in Righteousness

Once Sayyidah Maryam ('alaihas salaam) was weaned, her mother, Hannah, wrapped her in blankets and proceeded with her to the masjid. As she had dedicated this child to the worship of Allah Ta'ala, she made her over to the devout worshippers residing in the masjid. All of them were eager to have the honour of raising her.

Nabi Zakariyya ('alaihis salaam) was the Nabi of the time, and he also wished to have the privilege of raising Sayyidah Maryam ('alaihas salaam), especially as she was his niece (his wife was the sister of Hannah). Hence, to decide who would have the honour of raising her, they decided to draw lots.

They all gathered their pens together at a certain place and a young boy was instructed to draw a pen from the lot. When this was done, the pen drawn turned out to be that of Nabi Zakariyya ('alaihis salaam).

The worshippers asked Nabi Zakariyya ('alaihis salaam) to draw lots for a second time, and he agreed. On this occasion, they all cast their pens into the river, agreeing that the decision would be in favour of the pen which miraculously flowed against the current. When this was done, it was the pen of Nabi Zakariyya ('alaihis salaam) which flowed against the current, while all the other pens flowed with the current.

Finally, the worshippers requested Nabi Zakariyya ('alaihis salaam) to draw lots for a third time. Again they cast their pens into the river, agreeing that the decision would now be in favour of the pen which flowed with the current, while the other pens flowed against the current. Once more, it was the pen of Nabi Zakariyya ('alaihis salaam) which flowed with the current, while the other pens went against the current. In this manner, Nabi Zakariyya ('alaihis salaam) was chosen as being the most worthy of raising her. Allah Ta'ala endorsed him and allowed him to raise Sayyidah Maryam ('alaihas salaam) as he was the Nabi and as his wife was the aunt of Sayyidah Maryam ('alaihas salaam),

Nabi Zakariyya ('alaihis salaam) then arranged a special area which was exclusive for Sayyidah Maryam ('alaihas salaam) where she would remain and engage in worshipping Allah Ta'ala throughout the day and night. She exerted herself in worship to such an extent that her worship was regarded as proverbial among the Banu Israaeel.

(Surah Aal 'Imraan v44 and Al-Bidaayah wan Nihaayah vol. 2, pg. 65)

Lessons:

❀ When Allah Ta'ala decrees that a person will receive something, he will most definitely receive it. Be it a child, sustenance or anything else, everything is in the control of Allah Ta'ala. If we secure His help, we will be able to overcome any challenge.

❀ In raising Sayyidah Maryam ('alaihas salaam), Nabi Zakariyya ('alaihis salaam) ensured that she was in seclusion, as solitude is conducive to worshipping Allah Ta'ala. Since the objective of solitude is to allow a person to achieve peace of mind and remain focused, we should try to achieve the same result by eliminating all unnecessary distractions from our lives. At present, perhaps the most destructive distractions are social media, novels, etc., all of which are made available through the internet. Hence, our 'seclusion' and that of our families can be achieved by disconnecting from the unnecessary usage of the internet so that we may connect with Allah Ta'ala.

The 'Produce' of Piety

Allah Ta'ala bestowed Sayyidah Maryam ('alaihas salaam) with His divine acceptance and blessed her to receive an upbringing that was excellent and outstanding. With regards to her upbringing, Allah Ta'ala mentions in the Quraan Majeed, "And her Rabb accepted her graciously and made her grow excellently."

One aspect of "making her grow excellently" is that she received an exceptional upbringing of piety and righteousness. Hence, from a young age, she always remained engaged in the worship and obedience of Allah Ta'ala.

On account of this very piety and purity which Allah Ta'ala had blessed her with, Allah Ta'ala instructed the angels to announce to her, "O Maryam ('alaihas salaam)! Indeed Allah Ta'ala has selected you, purified you and chosen you above all women."

As she was in the care of Nabi Zakariyya ('alaihis salaam), he would often enter the special area in which Sayyidah Maryam ('alaihas salaam) secluded herself while engaging in the worship of Allah Ta'ala. To his surprise, Nabi Zakariyya ('alaihis salaam) would find that she had fruit that was out of season! In winter, she would be enjoying the fruit of summer, and in summer, she would be enjoying the fruit of winter. Nabi Zakariyya ('alaihis salaam) asked her, "O Maryam ('alaihas salaam)! From where does this come to you?" She replied, "It is from Allah. Indeed, Allah provides sustenance to whom He pleases without measure."

At that moment, despite being advanced in age, Nabi Zakariyya ('alaihis salaam) desired to be blessed with a child. Hence, he turned to Allah Ta'ala in du'aa and supplicated saying, "O the One Who blessed Maryam ('alaihas salaam) with fruit that was out of season, bless me with a child, even though I have passed the 'season' (age) of fatherhood."

Allah Ta'ala accepted the du'aa of Nabi Zakariyya ('alaihis salaam) and eventually blessed him with a son who was Nabi Yahya ('alaihis salaam).

(Surah Aal 'Imraan v37-39 & v42, Bayaanul Quraan vol. 1, pg. 223, Tafseer Ibni Katheer vol. 2, pg. 344 and Al-Bidaayah wan Nihaayah vol. 2, pg. 65)

Lessons:

🌹   Just as every parent wishes that their child will have good and healthy physical development, they should have an even greater concern for the Deeni and imaani upbringing and development of their children. In this regard, it is incumbent for them to constantly make du'aa for their children's Deen and imaan – if not after every salaah, then at least once a day. Additionally, they must ensure that their children attend a good maktab madrasah and daily ta'leem is conducted in the home.

🌹   Allah Ta'ala alone is the sole Sustainer of every creation. When we have firm imaan and conviction in this, we will turn to Allah Ta'ala and believe that it is only in obeying Him and pleasing Him that we will gain barakah (blessings) in our sustenance. Furthermore, just as Allah Ta'ala sent fruit that was out of season for Sayyidah Maryam ('alaihas salaam) while she was within her chamber, Allah Ta'ala can easily arrange and see to our sustenance while we remain within our homes seeking His pleasure.

🌹   The power of du'aa should never be forgotten or overlooked. Allah Ta'ala, in the blink of an eye, can literally make our dreams come true. Remain in the obedience of Allah Ta'ala and turn to Him for your every need.

The Preparation of Piety

Allah Ta'ala instructed the angels to give Sayyidah Maryam ('alaihas salaam) the glad tidings that she would give birth to a son named 'Isa ('alaihis salaam) without the medium of a father. The angels also gave her the glad tidings that this son would be the Nabi of Allah Ta'ala who would invite people towards Him while still a child. However, Sayyidah Maryam ('alaihas salaam) was instructed to exert herself in 'ibaadah so that she would become worthy of this great favour and bounty of Allah Ta'ala. Hence, she exerted herself in 'ibaadah and performed salaah to such an extent that her legs would become swollen.

Sayyidah Maryam ('alaihas salaam) would only leave Masjidul Aqsa when she was impure or when she had a need to fulfill. Once, while she was out, Allah Ta'ala sent Jibreel ('alaihis salaam) to her in the form of a man. As soon as she saw him, out of her extreme purity, chastity and shame, she exclaimed, "I seek the protection of the Most Merciful from you! If you possess taqwa (then do not come close to me)!" Jibreel ('alaihis salaam) assured her that he was an angel sent to her by Allah Ta'ala to bless her with a child. She asked, "How will I give birth to a son whereas no man has touched me (I am unmarried) and I am not unchaste?" Jibreel ('alaihis salaam) replied, "So it will be. Your Rabb has said, 'It is easy for me.'" Jibreel ('alaihis salaam) then blew into her collar through which Allah Ta'ala caused Nabi 'Isa ('alaihis salaam) to be conceived.

(Surah Aal 'Imraan v45-46, Surah Maryam v16-21, Tafseer Ibni Katheer vol. 2, pg. 346 and Al-Bidaayah wan Nihaayah vol. 2, pgs. 67, 73 & 74)

Lessons:

❀ Allah Ta'ala had honoured Sayyidah Maryam ('alaihas salaam) above all the women of the world to be the mother of Nabi 'Isa ('alaihis salaam) without the medium of a father. However, in order to become worthy of this bounty, she was instructed to exert herself in 'ibaadah. Similarly, Allah Ta'ala loves all His servants and wishes to bless them and shower His favours upon them. However, the general system of Allah Ta'ala is that He blesses His servants when they strive and show that they are eager for His blessings. Hence, together with making du'aa to Allah Ta'ala for Him to bless us, we have to exert ourselves in His 'ibaadah and in acquiring His pleasure.

❀ As soon as a strange man had come close to Sayyidah Maryam ('alaihas salaam), she sought the protection of Allah Ta'ala and reminded the man to adopt taqwa. This is the automatic and spontaneous reaction of a person who possesses hayaa (shame and modesty) – that they are always on their guard and are wary of non-mahrams coming close to them or approaching them.

Pleased with His Decree

Sayyidah Maryam ('alaihas salaam) realized that her conceiving Nabi 'Isa ('alaihis salaam) was a test for her, as people would notice that she was expecting and would ask who had fathered the child. However, she placed her trust in Allah Ta'ala and accepted that this was His decision.

The first person to notice that Sayyidah Maryam ('alaihas salaam) was expecting was her cousin, Yusuf bin Ya'qoob Najjaar. Being well aware of her piety and chastity knowing that she was unmarried, he was extremely surprised to see that she was expecting a child.

He thus asked her, "O Maryam ('alaihas salaam)! Is it possible for a plant to grow without a seed first being planted?" She replied, "Yes! After all, who created the very first plant?" He next asked her, "Is it possible for a tree to grow without water and rain?" She replied, "Yes! After all, who created the first tree?" Finally, he asked, "Can a child be born without a father?" She replied, "Yes! Allah Ta'ala created Nabi Aadam ('alaihis salaam) without a mother or a father." She then informed him that Allah Ta'ala had given her the glad tidings of being the mother of Nabi 'Isa ('alaihis salaam) without the intermediary of any father.

When Sayyidah Maryam ('alaihas salaam) would be in solitude, Nabi 'Isa ('alaihis salaam) would converse with her and speak to her from the womb, and when she would be among people, he would engage in reciting tasbeeh.

(Al-Bidaayah wan Nihaayah vol. 2, pgs. 73-75)

Lesson:

🌼 We should never desire or ask to be tested by Allah Ta'ala. However, if He has decreed a certain test for us, be it an illness, financial difficulty or any other test, then we should place our trust in Him and be happy with His decision. We should never question Allah Ta'ala, but should turn to Him in du'aa saying, "O Allah! Since You have given me this test, and I am weak, You assist me to pass this test and secure Your happiness."

Maintaining Modesty

Sayyidah Maryam ('alaihas salaam) bore Nabi 'Isa ('alaihis salaam) for the normal period of pregnancy. Thereafter, when her labour commenced, she went alone to the jungle, far away from people, to give birth to her child. As it was difficult for her to sit or stand, due to the severe labour pains, she used a date palm as a support.

This was indeed a great test for Sayyidah Maryam ('alaihas salaam). She was all alone with nobody to assist her. She was in pain, had no food or drink with her, and she anticipated that people would accuse her of being unchaste and committing fornication. In this state of desperation, she exclaimed, "If only I had died before this and was totally forgotten!" To console her, Allah Ta'ala sent Jibreel ('alaihis salaam) to her. He stood away from her, on an area lower than where she stood and said, "Do not grieve! Allah Ta'ala has provided a stream below you. Shake the trunk of the date palm and it will drop fresh dates for you."

In this manner, Allah Ta'ala made divine arrangements for Sayyidah Maryam ('alaihas salaam). **On her command, the stream would flow, and on her command, it would cease.** Similarly, another miracle was that the date palm bore fruit for her to eat, although it was not the season for dates.

After the period of nifaas (postnatal bleeding) had elapsed, approximately forty days later, Sayyidah Maryam ('alaihas salaam) returned to the people carrying Nabi 'Isa ('alaihis salaam). As soon as they saw her, they began to rebuke and chastise her, as she had born a child out of wedlock. They questioned how she could have stooped to such behaviour, whereas she hailed from the most pious of families.

Placing her complete reliance on Allah Ta'ala, Sayyidah Maryam ('alaihas salaam) remained silent and gestured towards her infant child. The people thought that she was mocking them, as a baby cannot speak. However, as a miracle, Allah Ta'ala allowed Nabi 'Isa ('alaihis salaam) to speak and he informed them that he was the Nabi of Allah Ta'ala. In this manner, the name and reputation of Sayyidah Maryam ('alaihas salaam) was preserved.

(Al-Bidaayah wan Nihaayah vol. 2, pgs. 74-78, Tafseerul Madaarik vol. 2, pg. 37 and Ma'aariful Quraan vol. 6, pgs. 22-28)

Lessons:

❀ **When people possessed shame and modesty, they frowned on indecent behaviour.** Today, with the surge of immodesty, people regard dating and other illicit relationships to be the norm. **This shows how far we have drifted from the values of Islam.** Sayyidah Maryam ('alaihas salaam) preferred to be dead rather than to be accused of indecent and unchaste behaviour.

❀ **When a believer leads a life of piety and chastity, has a strong link and relationship with Allah Ta'ala and places his reliance and trust in Him,** then Allah Ta'ala assists him in his hour of need and comes to his rescue.

The Recipe to Raise Pious Offspring

When Sayyidah Maryam ('alaihas salaam) was confronted by the people and accused of being unchaste, she gestured towards Nabi 'Isa ('alaihis salaam) who was an infant. As a miracle, Allah Ta'ala allowed Nabi 'Isa ('alaihis salaam) to speak. He raised his index finger and addressed the people.

The very first thing that Nabi 'Isa ('alaihis salaam) told them was, "I am the slave of Allah Ta'ala." In this way, he clearly declared that he was the slave of Allah Ta'ala and not the son of

Allah Ta'ala. He then informed them that Allah Ta'ala would reveal a divine book to him and make him a Nabi. By telling the people that he would become the Nabi of Allah Ta'ala, the people understood that his mother was innocent of any immorality and her name was thus cleared.

Nabi 'Isa ('alaihis salaam) then declared, "Allah Ta'ala has made me blessed, wherever I may be." In this context, when Nabi 'Isa ('alaihis salaam) mentioned 'blessed', it referred to the blessing of encouraging people towards righteous works and preventing them from committing evil deeds.

Nabi 'Isa ('alaihis salaam) then said, "Allah Ta'ala has enjoined on me salaah and zakaat as long as I am alive." Zakaat refers to 'purity' – of both wealth (through discharging zakaat and giving optional charity) and of the soul through purifying one's character of evil habits and traits.

Nabi 'Isa ('alaihis salaam) finally mentioned to the people that Allah Ta'ala had made him obedient and kind to his mother, and Allah Ta'ala had not made him harsh and rude, and he would not break the commands of Allah Ta'ala in any way.

(Tafseerul Madaarik vol. 2, pg. 38, Tafseer Ibni Katheer vol. 5, pg. 225, Al-Bidaayah wan Nihaayah vol. 2, pg. 79)

Lessons:

🌸   The qualities that Nabi 'Isa ('alaihis salaam) mentioned as a child are the same qualities that we should all strive to instil in our children. These are:

- Complete submission before Allah Ta'ala and His commands, as we are all His slaves.

- The effort to engage them in works of righteousness such as inviting people towards good and preventing them from evil, as this, in reality, is a great blessing and favour of Allah Ta'ala.

- To instil the importance of salaah in their hearts so that they never neglect any salaah, and to ensure that they strive for purity in wealth and in character.

- The children must be taught to respect, honour and serve their parents and seniors. They must be raised to be civilized and dignified and to behave respectfully and not in a harsh or rude manner.

🌸   In order to instil these qualities within our children, parents will have to first acquire these qualities themselves. Thereafter, they will become practical role models and examples for their children to emulate. Additionally, we should all make du'aa on a regular basis that Allah Ta'ala bless us with pious, obedient offspring who will please us as well as Allah Ta'ala.

Loyal to the Last

There was once a group of people who were suffering from a certain calamity. One of them approached Wahb bin Munabbih (rahimahullah) and asked, "O Abu 'Abdillah! Have you ever heard of a calamity or punishment that is worse and more severe than the calamity which we are suffering at present?" Wahb (rahimahullah) replied, "If you compare the difficulty that you are suffering and the difficulties that were experienced by the people of the past, you would realize that your difficulty compared to theirs is like smoke compared to fire!"

To illustrate the point, Wahb (rahimahullah) narrated the following incident:

There lived a woman in the Banu Israaeel who had seven sons. One day, the king of the time, who would force people to consume pork, summoned her together with her sons. When they were brought before him, he called the eldest son forward, presented some pork to him, and commanded him, "Eat this pork." The eldest son resolutely replied, "I will never eat something which Allah Ta'ala has declared haraam (forbidden)!" The king thus gave the command for the boy to be dismembered (his limbs be cut off, one by one), causing him to pass away.

The king then summoned the next son and ordered him, "Eat the pork." He too refused and replied, "I will never eat something which Allah Ta'ala has declared haraam!" The king thus ordered for a copper cauldron to be brought and filled with oil. He had a fire lit beneath and once the oil was boiling, the boy was cast into the boiling cauldron on his orders where he died.

The king then summoned the third son and instructed him to eat the pork. However, the third son fearlessly responded, "You are disgraced, weak and insignificant before Allah Ta'ala, so how can I obey you and disobey Allah Ta'ala by consuming that which He has made haraam?" The king laughed and remarked to those present, "Do you know why he is insulting me in this manner? He wishes to anger me so that I will kill him swiftly, but that will definitely prove to be his mistake (as I will do the opposite)!" Having said this, he instructed that the boy be skinned alive. First, the skin was peeled from his neck, then from his head and face, until the skin was peeled from his entire body, causing him to die.

The king then proceeded to kill the remaining brothers, using a different form of torture to end the life of each one, until only the youngest brother remained. Seeing the boy and his mother, the king addressed her and said, "It pains me to have seen you undergo this suffering. Take your son, and when you are alone with him, convince him to eat just one morsel of pork. If he does so, he will be allowed to live."

The mother agreed, and when she was alone with her son, she addressed him thus, "O my beloved son! Do you know that while I had a right over each of your brothers, I have a double right over you? The reason is that I had suckled each of your brothers for two years. However, since your father passed away while I was still expecting you, I felt even more attachment to you. Due to this feeling of sympathy for you, and due to your weakness, I suckled you for four years (as was perhaps permissible in their sharee'ah). I thus ask you in the name of Allah Ta'ala, and by the right that I have over you, that you never allow the point to come where you consume that which Allah Ta'ala has declared haraam. Do not meet your brothers in the Hereafter in the condition that you are not with them."

Hearing this, the son exclaimed, "All praise is due to Allah Ta'ala who enabled you to say these words to me! It was my fear that you would try to convince me to consume that which Allah Ta'ala has declared haraam!"

The mother then returned to the king with her son and said, "Here he is, I have spoken to him and convinced him." The king thus instructed him to eat, but the son refused and staunchly declared, "I will not consume that which Allah Ta'ala has made unlawful!" The king then gave the command for him to be killed, causing him to join his brothers by sharing their fate.

Finally, the king said to the mother, "I find myself pitying you, after the suffering that I have seen you undergo today! What is wrong with you? Eat one morsel! Then I will do with you as you please and give you whatever you wish so that you may live comfortably." The mother retorted, "You want me to mourn my sons and disobey Allah Ta'ala at the same time? I do not wish to live after them if it entails me doing this (as I will then suffer a double tragedy – the death of my sons and disobeying Allah Ta'ala). I will never consume that which Allah Ta'ala has declared haraam." The king thus had her killed as well, uniting her with her sons in the Hereafter.

('Uyoonul Hikaayaat pg. 27)

Lessons:

❀ It was only one thing that prompted the mother and her seven sons to behave in the manner they did – imaan. When a person's imaan is strong, his conviction in Allah Ta'ala and Jannah is so strong that he will not hesitate to sacrifice his life to please Allah Ta'ala. On the contrary, when imaan is weak, we will not be able to make even small sacrifices such as giving up sin and refraining from unlawful.

❀ The youngest son was raised without a father, yet his imaan was so strong that he stared death in the face and did not flinch. This could have only been the result of his mother's upbringing and attention. Similarly, every mother (and father as well) should make an effort to strengthen the imaan of their children and connect them to Allah Ta'ala. Conducting daily ta'leem in the home is an easy method to achieve this.

❀ Just as a person with an allergy cannot consume food which contains his allergen, similarly a believer cannot consume unlawful. If he consumes unlawful in any form (haraam food as well as anything acquired through unlawful wealth), it will cause his imaan to have an allergic reaction - weakening and damaging it.

The Fruit of Charity and Fire of Jealousy

There was once an evil king who threatened his subjects announcing, "If any person gives anything in charity, I will ensure that I have both his hands amputated!"

Thereafter, it so happened that a man approached a certain woman and begged her saying, "Please give me something in charity!" The woman responded, "How can I give you charity when the king is cutting off the hands of all those who give charity?" The man implored her saying, "I beg you to give me something for the sake of Allah!" The woman finally relented and gave him two loaves of bread as charity. However, when the news reached the king, he sent for this woman and had both her hands amputated.

After some time had passed, the king said to his mother, "Find me a beautiful woman whom I can marry." His mother replied, "There is a woman who is so beautiful that I have never seen beauty such as hers before. However, her beauty is marred by one severe defect." The king enquired, "What is it?" His mother answered, "Both her hands are amputated."

Nevertheless, the king sent for her, and on seeing her, was completely besotted as she was extremely beautiful. He sent her a proposal via his mother who said, "The king would like to marry you. (Do you accept his proposal)?" She replied in the affirmative, and they married soon thereafter. On marrying her, the king showed her much honour, kindness and care.

After some time, it so happened that an enemy of the king launched an attack against his land, compelling the king to march out and fight. While away, he wrote a letter to his mother, requesting her to look after his wife and take good care of her.

However, as the messenger was delivering the letter, he first encountered the other wives of the king. They became jealous of her and intercepted the letter. They then completely changed its message and in the king's name, they wrote to his mother saying, "Check on this wife of mine, for information has reached me that numerous men are fornicating with her. Ensure that you expel her from the palace."

When the king's mother received the letter, she wrote in reply, "This is a lie. She is a woman of loyalty and honesty." However, while carrying the letter, the messenger again encountered the other wives of the king. Once again, they took the letter from him and changed the message saying, "She is a shameless woman who has given birth to a boy (from her illicit activities)."

When the king received this fabricated message, he wrote to his mother saying, "Tie the child to her neck, beat her, and expel her from the palace into the desert." On receiving the letter, the king's mother read it to the wife and did as requested, and accordingly, the wife and her child were abandoned in the wilderness.

Helpless and alone, the mother began to walk with her child on her shoulders, until she came to a river. Since she was thirsty, she went towards it to drink water. However, as she knelt down to drink, the child fell from her neck into the water and drowned.

Overcome by grief, the woman began to weep (over her loss and her pitiable plight). In this state, she suddenly saw two men approaching. They asked her, "Why are you crying?" She replied, "My son was on my neck, and I do not have hands, so he fell into the water and drowned." They asked her, "Do you want us to return your son to you?" When she replied in the affirmative, they made du'aa to Allah Ta'ala, and before long, her son emerged from the river.

The two men then asked her, "Would you like your hands to be returned to you?" She agreed, and the two men again made du'aa, after which her hands were restored to her.

The two men then asked her, "Do you know who we are?" When she replied that she did not know, they said, "We are the two loaves of bread that you had given in charity."

(Hilyatul Awliyaa vol. 3, pg. 102 and Kitaabul Birri was Silah - Ibnul Jawzi [rahimahullah] #379)

Lessons:

❀ Charity has the special effect of drawing the mercy and assistance of Allah Ta'ala. Hence, we should endeavour to give sadaqah daily. We should give whatever we are able to manage, and should not regard any amount as too small – even if it is just R2. Often, through the blessing of our charity, Allah Ta'ala diverts certain calamities from us that were destined to befall us, or He sends us His special assistance in our hour of need.

❀ When we receive information – especially negative information – regarding people, we should ignore it if it does not relate to us, as this information may be gheebah (backbiting) or buhtaan (slander). If the information does concern us (e.g. it relates to our spouse, child or someone over whom we have some responsibility or influence) then we MUST ensure that we verify the information before accepting it and taking a decision. In many cases, to further their own agendas, people convey information out of context, or fail to narrate the full story, or exaggerate, or even fabricate. Don't be gullible and take every person at his word, as the day may then come when you will be forced to eat your words.

❀ When a person is consumed by jealousy, he finds no happiness or joy in life, nor is he prepared to allow others to experience happiness or joy. His own life is ruined and he wishes to ruin the lives of others. Hence, the outcome of jealousy is that one spends his life 'burning' within, over the prosperity of others, and he will burn in the Hereafter as well, as punishment for the serious sin of jealousy.

Sustained from His Unseen Treasures

Sayyiduna Abu Hurairah (radhiyallahu 'anhu) reports the following incident from Rasulullah (sallallahu 'alaihi wasallam):

From the people of the past, there was a husband and wife who were extremely poor. On one occasion, the husband arrived home from a journey. Suffering from the pangs of hunger, he asked his wife, "Do you have any food?" (Seeing him in this pitiable state, she did not have the heart to tell him that there was no food, so) she replied, "Yes, glad tidings, for the sustenance of Allah Ta'ala will soon come to you!"

(The husband's hunger was so severe that he could not wait, and) he thus demanded the food immediately. He said to her, "What is the matter with you? Go and see if you have any food or not!" His wife (calmly) responded, "In a few moments! We have hope in the mercy of Allah Ta'ala!"

Eventually, when the husband could wait no longer, he said to his wife, "What is wrong with you? Go look for some bread! If you have some, bring it for me to eat, for I cannot tolerate the hunger anymore and I am suffering!" His wife responded, "Yes, the food in the oven will soon be ready! Don't be hasty!"

After some time passed, during which the husband remained silent, and she anticipated that her husband would again ask her to see if there was any food in the house, she thought to herself, "Why don't I go and look in the oven?" With this in mind, she went to the oven, and (to her absolute astonishment,) she found it filled with meat, and she found that her mill was grinding grain into flour! She thus took the flour from the mill, lifting it and emptying it out, and removed the meat from the oven.

After narrating this incident, Rasulullah (sallallahu 'alaihi wasallam) mentioned, "I take an oath by that Being in Whose control lies the life of Abul Qaasim (sallallahu 'alaihi wasallam)! If she had taken the flour from the mill, without lifting and emptying it, it would have continued grinding and producing flour until the Day of Qiyaamah."

(Musnad Ahmad #9464)

Lessons:

The wife understood that her husband was starving and exhausted, as he had just arrived from a journey. Hence, she tried, within the best of her understanding and ability, to lessen his burden and did not tell him that there was no food in the house. She displayed a remarkable sense of consideration and compassion for her husband. It is thus imperative for one spouse to consider the feelings and mood of the other. When we need to discuss a sensitive issue with our partners, we should ensure that the time, place and manner are all suitable.

🌸 Allah Ta'ala is the Sole Provider for the entire creation. Just as Allah Ta'ala provides with means (e.g. through a person working and earning), Allah Ta'ala also provides without means. In essence, we must have the complete conviction that it is Allah Ta'ala alone who provides, and our sustenance has been preordained. If we have this mindset, we will never be tempted to stretch our hand to impermissible wealth or impermissible food. Likewise, we will be content with what we have, as we understand that it was preordained for us, and no effort of our own could have changed what we received.

🌸 If we have any problem, we should turn to Allah Ta'ala and place our trust in Him. Allah Ta'ala is All-Powerful and has complete control over everything. He can easily assist us from the unseen and bless us with ease after our difficulty. All that is required is that we lead lives pleasing to Him and place our trust in Him.

Era of the Sahaabah
(radhiyallahu 'anhum)

First Impressions...

Sayyiduna 'Abdullah bin Mas'ood (radhiyallahu 'anhu) once mentioned the following, describing his first encounter with Muslims and his first impression of Islam:

"I came to Makkah Mukarramah, accompanying my uncles, with the intention of purchasing some commodities. Since we also required some 'itr (perfume), we were directed to the uncle of Nabi (sallallahu 'alaihi wasallam), Sayyiduna 'Abbaas (radhiyallahu 'anhu).

While seated with Sayyiduna 'Abbaas (radhiyallahu 'anhu) at the well of Zam-Zam, a man suddenly entered the Haram from the door of Safaa. His skin was fair with a tinge of redness in his complexion. His hair was long and wavy and he had a thick beard. His eyes were most outstanding and his teeth were white and shining. (His beauty was such that) he resembled the full moon. On his right was a young, handsome boy, and behind them was a woman who had concealed her beauty.

The three of them proceeded to the Hajr Aswad (black stone), performed tawaaf of the Ka'bah, and then worshipped Allah Ta'ala in a unique manner which we had never before witnessed.

We asked 'Abbaas (radhiyallahu 'anhu), 'Is this a new religion?' 'Abbaas (radhiyallahu 'anhu) replied, 'Yes, this is my nephew, Muhammad (sallallahu 'alaihi wasallam). The young boy is 'Ali (radhiyallahu 'anhu), and the woman is Khadeejah (radhiyallahu 'anha). They are the only three people on the surface of the earth who are worshipping Allah Ta'ala in this way.'"

(Taareekh Ibni 'Asaakir vol. 33, pg. 67 and Tabraani - Majma'uz Zawaaid #15257)

Lessons:

❀ When describing his first impression of Islam and Muslims, Sayyiduna 'Abdullah bin Mas'ood (radhiyallahu 'anhu) specifically mentioned, "behind them was a woman who had concealed her beauty." This was in the very beginning of Islam, before the majority of the injunctions of Islam (e.g. fasting, haj, etc.) were revealed. Hence, we understand that the quality of hayaa (chastity, modesty and bashfulness) has always been a central and integral part of Islam.

❀ Despite being in a land and era where ignorance and immoral practices abounded, hijaab and niqaab were still upheld, thus creating a lasting impression on Sayyiduna 'Abdullah bin Mas'ood (radhiyallahu 'anhu). Therefore, in this day and age, where immorality and shamelessness abound once more, we must try our best to uphold the integral qualities of hayaa and conceal our beauty with hijaab and niqaab, as this is how we will safeguard our imaan and Deen.

"Are You Blind?"

Sayyidah Ummu Salamah (radhiyallahu 'anha) says,

"I was once in the blessed presence of Rasulullah (sallallahu 'alaihi wasallam) while Maimoonah (radhiyallahu 'anha) was also present. While we were with Rasulullah (sallallahu 'alaihi wasallam), 'Abdullah bin Ummi Maktoom (radhiyallahu 'anhu) arrived, and this was after the law of hijaab (purdah) was revealed.

"When 'Abdullah (radhiyallahu 'anhu) arrived, Nabi (sallallahu 'alaihi wasallam) instructed us, 'Adopt hijaab from him.' We replied, 'O Rasul of Allah (sallallahu 'alaihi wasallam)! Is he not a blind man who can neither see us nor recognize us?' Rasulullah (sallallahu 'alaihi wasallam) responded, 'Are the two of you blind? Can the two of you not see him?'"

(Sunan Abi Dawood #4112)

Lessons:

❀ The blessed wives of Rasulullah (sallallahu 'alaihi wasallam) were the purest of women, living in the purest of ages, in the purest of presences – the presence of Rasulullah (sallallahu 'alaihi wasallam) – and the man who entered, over and above being blind, was a Sahaabi and was thus from the purest of men. Despite the level of purity that prevailed, Rasulullah (sallallahu 'alaihi wasallam) still instructed his respected wives to adopt hijaab in the presence of this Sahaabi, as there is more precaution in this.

When Rasulullah (sallallahu 'alaihi wasallam) commanded his respected wives to adopt hijaab and not look at this blind Sahaabi in the situation of pristine purity described above, we can well imagine the law that applies to us! After all, we live in an age and environment wherein evil, immorality, shamelessness, lewdness and lust prevail. Sadly, we have drifted far from the sunnah of Rasulullah (sallallahu 'alaihi wasallam)! Many of our functions, weddings, and even 'Islamic' events are held without segregation between males and females.

Sayyidah 'Aaishah (radhiyallahu 'anha)

The Most Beloved of the Most Beloved

Allah Ta'ala had blessed multiple women with the honour of becoming the Azwaaj Mutahharaat (pure and chaste wives of Rasulullah [sallallahu 'alaihi wasallam]). However, from all the Azwaaj Mutahharaat, perhaps the one who is most well-known is Sayyidah 'Aaishah (radhiyallahu 'anha).

Not only was Sayyidah 'Aaishah (radhiyallahu 'anha) the most beloved of the Azwaaj Mutahharaat to our most beloved Rasul (sallallahu 'alaihi wasallam), but among all his wives, she was blessed with many special virtues that were unique to her alone.

Sayyidah 'Aaishah (radhiyallahu 'anha) once mentioned the following to the other Azwaaj Mutahharaat:

"I was favoured over you with ten special blessings – and I do not say this with pride (but rather to express gratitude to Allah

Ta'ala. These ten special blessings are that) I was the most beloved to Rasulullah (sallallahu 'alaihi wasallam) from all his wives and my father was the most beloved to him (from all the Sahaabah [radhiyallahu 'anhum]).

Rasulullah (sallallahu 'alaihi wasallam) married me as a virgin, whereas he did not marry any other woman who was a virgin besides me. Rasulullah (sallallahu 'alaihi wasallam) married me at the age of seven, and I went to live with him when I was nine.

(When I was falsely accused of fornication,) my exoneration and the declaration of my innocence descended from the sky (as revelation to be recorded in the Quraan Majeed).

When Rasulullah (sallallahu 'alaihi wasallam) was in his final illness, he asked his wives permission saying, 'It is difficult for me to continue moving between your homes (giving each of you your due turn). Hence, allow me to remain with one of you.' When Rasulullah (sallallahu 'alaihi wasallam) said that, Ummu Salamah (radhiyallahu 'anha) said, 'We understand that you wish to stay at the home of 'Aaishah (radhiyallahu 'anha). We have given you permission to do so (as this is what pleases you).'

The final thing to be placed in the blessed mouth of Rasulullah (sallallahu 'alaihi wasallam) in the world was my saliva. A miswaak was brought to Rasulullah (sallallahu 'alaihi wasallam), and he asked me to chew it for him and soften it for him, which I did (and he then used the miswaak, due to which my saliva was in his blessed mouth when he departed from this world).

(Finally,) Rasulullah (sallallahu 'alaihi wasallam) departed from this world while reclining on me, (with his blessed head) between my lap and my chest, and he was buried in my home."

(Siyaru Aa'laamin Nubalaa vol. 2, pg. 147)

Sayyidah 'Aaishah (radhiyallahu 'anha) was blessed with many other special virtues and bounties by Allah Ta'ala, which indicate to the high rank and status that Allah Ta'ala had blessed her with.

Hereunder are glimpses into the blessed life of this outstanding personality so that she may serve as an inspiration to us all.

Spontaneous Modesty

The Expedition of Banul Mustaliq occurred during the month of Sha'baan 5 A.H. Together with the Sahaabah (radhiyallahu 'anhum) who accompanied Rasulullah (sallallahu 'alaihi wasallam) on this expedition, Rasulullah (sallallahu 'alaihi wasallam) also took his respected wife, Sayyidah 'Aaishah (radhiyallahu 'anha) along with him.

On the return journey, they had halted for the night at a place close to Madeenah Munawwarah. Prior to the time of departure, Sayyidah 'Aaishah (radhiyallahu 'anha) went some distance away from the camp site to take care of her physical needs. When she returned, she realized that her necklace had fallen off and therefore went back in search of it. In the process of finding her necklace, she was delayed, and upon returning to the camp site, she found that the army had already departed.

Since Sayyidah 'Aaishah (radhiyallahu 'anha) was very light in weight at that time, the Sahaabah (radhiyallahu 'anhum) who had lifted the 'hawdaj' (a curtained carriage) and placed it on the camel's back did not even realize that she was not inside.

Sayyidah 'Aaishah (radhiyallahu 'anha) relates, "I proceeded to the place in which I had initially been, realizing that they would soon discover that I was missing and return for me. I then covered myself with my shawl, and fell asleep.

As per his own request, Safwaan bin Mu'attal (radhiyallahu 'anhu) was appointed by Rasulullah (sallallahu 'alaihi wasallam) to follow behind the army. Hence, when the army would depart, he would remain in the camp, performing salaah. After some time, he would follow behind the army, recovering lost items, such as a water skin or utensil that any person in the army had left behind, so that he could return it to the owner.

As Safwaan (radhiyallahu 'anhu) proceeded, he came to the place where I was, noticed the figure of a person sleeping, and recognized me (as the shawl had fallen from my face, while I was asleep). Safwaan (radhiyallahu 'anhu) was able to recognize me as he had seen me in the era before the laws of hijaab (purdah) were revealed.

As soon as he saw me, he loudly recited, 'innaa lillaahi wa innaa ilaihi raaji'oon', causing me to awaken. On awakening, my spontaneous reaction was to cover my face and conceal it from him. By Allah! We did not speak anything to one another, nor did I hear any word from him besides his reciting of 'innaa lillaah'.

He then brought his camel to me, made it kneel, and turned his face away, allowing me to climb onto the camel. He then led the camel, until we reached the army."

(Saheeh Bukhaari #4750 and Fat-hul Baari)

Lessons:

❀ Before she fell asleep, Sayyidah 'Aaishah (radhiyallahu 'anha) covered herself, and as soon as she awoke, her spontaneous reaction was to cover her face as well. The aspect of hijaab and purdah was so deeply ingrained in Sayyidah 'Aaishah (radhiyallahu 'anha) that it was her second nature. It is thus very clear that the Sahaabah (radhiyallahu 'anhum), despite the high level of their piety, purity of their hearts, and deep consciousness of Allah Ta'ala, did not regard the covering of the face to be a trivial matter or something insignificant. Rather they showed it utmost importance, as they knew that hayaa is directly linked to imaan.

❀ When Sayyiduna Safwaan (radhiyallahu 'anhu) discovered Sayyidah 'Aaishah (radhiyallahu 'anha), he woke her by loudly reciting 'innaa lillaahi wa innaa ilaihi raaji'oon', in order to avoid any direct conversation. When a Sahaabi exercised this level of caution when interacting with his 'mother' in a situation of dire necessity, due to her being a non-mahram, what level of caution should we be exercising, in a time that abounds with lust and illicit behaviour. While this applies to physical meetings and verbal conversations, it equally applies to interacting via social media platforms.

❦ Sayyiduna Safwaan (radhiyallahu 'anhu) had to fulfil the necessary duty of transporting Sayyidah 'Aaishah (radhiyallahu 'anha) back to the army, as he could not leave her alone in the wilderness. However, he did so with utmost hayaa. While she was climbing onto the camel, he turned away completely, **and after she was mounted on the camel, he did not walk beside her, but walked in front, where he could not see her.** In essence, both of them displayed the highest levels of hayaa and modesty, despite the difficult situation, thus setting the standard for the Ummah to follow.

Sublime Display of Submission

On one occasion, Sayyidah 'Aaishah (radhiyallahu 'anha) bought a cushion which was decorated with pictures of animate objects. When Rasulullah (sallallahu 'alaihi wasallam) arrived later, he noticed the cushion from the outside. Rasulullah (sallallahu 'alaihi wasallam) thus refrained from entering the home and remained standing in the doorway.

When Sayyidah 'Aaishah (radhiyallahu 'anha) saw Rasulullah (sallallahu 'alaihi wasallam) standing in the doorway with the signs of anger evident on his blessed face, she immediately exclaimed, "I repent to Allah Ta'ala and His Rasul (sallallahu 'alaihi wasallam)!"

To rectify her mistake and secure the pleasure of Allah Ta'ala, she then asked, "What sin did I commit?" In reply, Rasulullah (sallallahu 'alaihi wasallam) asked her regarding the cushion. She responded, "I bought it for you so that you may sit on it and rest against it." Rasulullah (sallallahu 'alaihi wasallam) then mentioned, "Indeed the people who made these pictures (of animate objects) will be punished on the Day of Qiyaamah and it will be said to them, 'Give life to the picture which you made!'" Rasulullah (sallallahu 'alaihi wasallam) also mentioned, "The angels (of mercy, blessings, protection, etc.) do not enter the home in which there are pictures (of animate objects)."

(Saheeh Bukhaari #2105)

Lessons:

❀ The extremely high level of submission and humility in our beloved mother, Sayyidah 'Aaishah (radhiyallahu 'anha), can be gauged by her response and reaction in the above incident. When she saw that Rasulullah (sallallahu 'alaihi wasallam) was displeased, then despite being unaware of her mistake, she immediately repented to Allah Ta'ala and Rasulullah (sallallahu 'alaihi wasallam). Only after expressing her remorse did she enquire as to what her mistake was so that she could rectify it. It is thus clear that her first priority was to please Allah Ta'ala and Rasulullah (sallallahu 'alaihi wasallam). If it had been one of us, then to appease our ego, we would have first become defensive and would have protested saying, "Why are you angry? What did I do?" Sayyidah 'Aaishah (radhiyallahu 'anha) however, displayed an exemplary level of submission and humility.

🌷 We should constantly try to identify our weaknesses and sins so that we may rectify ourselves and gain the pleasure of Allah Ta'ala. Furthermore, since we commit many sins unknowingly, we should engage in regular repentance for all our sins – those which we are aware of as well as those which we are unaware of.

🌷 We also learn from this incident not to assume that we know what is right and wrong. We could be mistaken or misunderstand, therefore we must always refer to and rely on those who are learned.

🌷 The sin of making pictures of animate objects and also keeping such pictures is extremely severe. We should totally abstain from this, whether the pictures are made through drawing, painting, taking photos, making videos, etc. If we are guilty of this sin, we should immediately repent and destroy the pictures that we have made or kept.

🌷 When pictures of animate objects are kept in the home, the angels of mercy are prevented from entering the home. Hence, by keeping such pictures with us, we deprive ourselves of the presence of these angels. As a result, we are deprived of Allah Ta'ala's mercy and blessings as well as the protection and du'aa of the angels.

The Resource that Remains

Sayyidah Naseekah (radhiyallahu 'anha) narrates the following:

I was once at the home of Sayyidah 'Aaishah (radhiyallahu 'anha) when she slaughtered a goat. While I was still there, Rasulullah (sallallahu 'alaihi wasallam) entered carrying a small stick in his blessed hand.

Rasulullah (sallallahu 'alaihi wasallam) placed the stick down and then entered the masjid where he performed two rakaats of salaah. Rasulullah (sallallahu 'alaihi wasallam) thereafter returned and lay down on his bed, asking Sayyidah 'Aaishah (radhiyallahu 'anha), "Is there anything to eat?"

Sayyidah 'Aaishah (radhiyallahu 'anha) immediately brought a platter of barley bread, together with a little tripe and the shoulder of the goat. She placed the platter before Rasulullah (sallallahu 'alaihi wasallam) and began to eat with him. As she began to bite from the tripe, she mentioned to Rasulullah (sallallahu 'alaihi wasallam), "We slaughtered a goat today, and we did not keep anything besides this (i.e. we gave the entire goat in sadaqah besides the portion that we are eating)."

When Rasulullah (sallallahu 'alaihi wasallam) heard this, he replied, "No! You actually kept the entire goat besides this (i.e. whatever has been given in sadaqah has actually been 'kept' as a reward in the Hereafter)."

In another narration, it is mentioned that Rasulullah (sallallahu 'alaihi wasallam) asked Sayyidah 'Aaishah (radhiyallahu 'anha), "Is there anything remaining from the goat that was slaughtered?" Sayyidah 'Aaishah (radhiyallahu 'anha) replied, "There is nothing remaining besides the shoulder." Rasulullah (sallallahu 'alaihi wasallam) replied, "The entire goat has remained, besides the shoulder (i.e. the reward for most of the goat, besides the shoulder, has remained in the Hereafter, as it was given in sadaqah)."

(Tabraani - Majma'uz Zawaaid #8055 and Sunan Tirmizi #2470)

Lessons:

❦ The hadeeth mentions that on certain occasions, three months would pass wherein the blessed household of Rasulullah (sallallahu 'alaihi wasallam) did not have anything to eat besides dates and water! Despite undergoing such difficulty and hunger, when they did acquire some meat, they kept very little for themselves and gave the rest in sadaqah. The Sahaabah (radhiyallahu 'anhum) were not consumed by the love of luxuries and wealth, but rather kept their focus on securing the rewards of the Hereafter.

❀ The only resource that will remain with a person on his journey to the Hereafter will be the rewards of his good actions. Hence, we should invest our time, energy and wealth into securing the rewards of the Hereafter.

❀ Rasulullah (sallallahu 'alaihi wasallam) would always turn the attention of the Sahaabah (radhiyallahu 'anhum) towards the Hereafter. Hence, even in the hadeeth above, Rasulullah (sallallahu 'alaihi wasallam) turned the attention of Sayyidah 'Aaishah (radhiyallahu 'anha) towards the reward of the sadaqah in the Hereafter. We should all try to turn our hearts to the eternal bounties of Jannah and strive accordingly.

Eat to Live, Not Live to Eat

In various ahaadeeth, Sayyidah 'Aaishah (radhiyallahu 'anha) explains the food of the household of Rasulullah (sallallahu 'alaihi wasallam).

In one narration, she mentions, "From the time Rasulullah (sallallahu 'alaihi wasallam) came to Madeenah Munawwarah, until the time he departed from this world, his household were never satiated with food prepared from wheat for three consecutive nights." *(Saheeh Bukhaari #5416)*

Likewise, in another narration she mentions, "At the time when Rasulullah (sallallahu 'alaihi wasallam) departed from this world, we would satiate our hunger with dates and water." *(Saheeh Bukaari #5383)*

Even after the demise of Rasulullah (sallallahu 'alaihi wasallam), Sayyidah 'Aaishah (radhiyallahu 'anha) maintained this level of simplicity. Hence, when wealth began to pour into Madeenah Munawwarah and large amounts of money would be sent to her, she never kept anything for herself. Instead, she hastened to spend it all in charity, emulating the blessed example of Rasulullah (sallallahu 'alaihi wasallam).

The nephew of Sayyidah 'Aaishah (radhiyallahu 'anha), 'Urwah bin Zubair (rahimahullah), mentions that on one occasion, Sayyiduna Mu'aawiyah (radhiyallahu 'anhu) sent 100 000 dirhams (silver coins) to her as a gift. On receiving the gift, she began to distribute it among the poor, until nothing remained. At that time, her freed slave, Sayyidah Bareerah (radhiyallahu 'anha), remarked, "You are fasting. Why did you not purchase some meat for us with (at least) one dirham?" Sayyidah 'Aaishah (radhiyallahu 'anha) replied, "Had I thought of it, I would have done so." *(Mustadrak Haakim #6745)*

Similarly, on another occasion, her nephew, Sayyiduna 'Abdullah bin Zubair (radhiyallahu 'anhuma), sent her two sacks, filled with money, as a gift. Contained in these sacks was wealth equal to approximately 180 000 dirhams. On receiving the gift, Sayyidah 'Aaishah (radhiyallahu 'anha) asked for a tray to be brought. She then (placed the money in the tray and) sat, distributing the money among the people. By that evening, none of the money remained.

Since Sayyidah 'Aaishah (radhiyallahu 'anha) was fasting, she called to her servant, "Please bring my iftaar (the food with which I will break my fast)." The servant obliged and presented her with some bread and olive oil. Observing this, her freed slave, Sayyidah Ummu Zarrah (radhiyallahu 'anha) remarked, "From the money you distributed today, could you not have used one dirham to purchase meat for us to eat when breaking our fast?" Sayyidah 'Aaishah (radhiyallahu 'anha) replied, "Do not reprimand me! If you had reminded me, I would have done so!" *(Sifatus Safwah vol. 1, pg. 318)*

Lessons:

❀ Food prepared from wheat (e.g. bread) is not an exclusive or exotic type of food. Rather, it is among the basic, staple foods. However, the simplicity and generosity of Rasulullah (sallallahu 'alaihi wasallam) and his blessed household was such that they voluntarily chose to spend all their wealth in the path of Allah Ta'ala, assisting others and securing the rewards of the Hereafter. Hence, they did not even have wheat bread to eat for three nights in a row. Rather, they would eat barley bread (which was cheaper) or satiate their hunger by eating dates (which were abundantly available) and drinking water.

❀ The effect of remaining in the blessed company of Rasulullah (sallallahu 'alaihi wasallam) was that even after his demise, his household emulated his blessed example. **They had** imbibed the values of generosity and simplicity to such an extent that they too voluntarily sacrificed the material possessions, for the sake of others, and sufficed on the simplest of foods.

When Sayyidah 'Aaishah (radhiyallahu 'anha) was asked as to why she had not purchased meat for her iftaar, she remarked that if it had occurred to her, or she had been reminded, she would have done so. In other words, although she was fasting, and had probably not eaten meat for many days, food was the furthest thing from her mind and she was not pining for meat. On the other hand, we constantly obsess over our food and our menu – even more so when we are fasting. In many ways, our lives actually revolve around our stomachs. However, as we can see from the above incidents, this was not the way of Rasulullah (sallallahu 'alaihi wasallam) and the Sahaabah (radhiyallahu 'anhum). They ate to live, not lived to eat.

Forgiven and Forgotten

As mentioned earlier, Sayyidah 'Aaishah (radhiyallahu 'anha) was mistakenly left behind when the army departed while returning from the expedition of Banul Mustaliq. When Sayyiduna Safwaan bin Mu'attal (radhiyallahu 'anhu) later discovered her waiting in the place where the Sahaabah (radhiyallahu 'anhum) had camped, he escorted her safely back to the army.

When they arrived at the army, the tongues of the hypocrites began to wag, and they spread the rumour that – Allah Ta'ala forbid! – Sayyidah 'Aaishah (radhiyallahu 'anha) had indulged in sin with Sayyiduna Safwaan (radhiyallahu 'anhu). In this manner, they falsely accused our beloved mother, Sayyidah 'Aaishah (radhiyallahu 'anha), of indecency (na'oozubillah). This incident is known as the incident of ifk (slander).

Unfortunately, although the hypocrites were responsible for starting the rumours, there were a few sincere Sahaabah (radhiyallahu 'anhum) who erred and also became unwittingly involved in speaking of these rumours. Among these Sahaabah (radhiyallahu 'anhum) was Sayyiduna Hassaan bin Thaabit (radhiyallahu 'anhu), the poet who would use his poetry to speak in defence of Rasulullah (sallallahu 'alaihi wasallam) when the disbelievers would mock at him.

After a period of time, during which Sayyidah 'Aaishah (radhiyallahu 'anha) suffered extreme anguish, as the stigma of the false rumour persisted, Allah Ta'ala Himself exonerated her and declared her innocence by revealing verses of the Quraan Majeed in her defence.

On one occasion, many years later, a nephew of Sayyidah 'Aaishah (radhiyallahu 'anha) began to speak ill of Sayyiduna Hassaan (radhiyallahu 'anhu) in her presence. When she heard the words of her nephew, she stopped him saying, "Do not speak ill of him, for he would defend Rasulullah (sallallahu 'alaihi wasallam) (by means of his poetry)."

(Saheeh Bukhaari #3531)

Lessons:

❦ This incident is clear testament to how clean the heart of Sayyidah 'Aaishah (radhiyallahu 'anha) was. Despite Sayyiduna Hassaan (radhiyallahu 'anhu) being among those who had erred and unwittingly assisted in spreading the rumour, she pardoned and forgave him. Furthermore, she did not only forgive, but even 'forgot', by thereafter defending him when her own nephew wished to speak ill of him. This forgiving nature and keeping a clean heart, free of malice and grudges, is the sunnah of Rasulullah (sallallahu 'alaihi wasallam) and hence, who could have learnt it better than Sayyidah 'Aaishah (radhiyallahu 'anha)?

❦ We should be extremely wary and cautious of all gossip and rumours – especially in the age of social media, when unfounded and unverified information abounds and rapidly circulates. If we become party to propagating a false rumour, we will be answerable by Allah Ta'ala. Hence, if the rumour is none of our business, let it stay that way. If it does pertain to us, we must verify it before accepting and acting on it.

Firm Faith in Allah

On one occasion, a beggar came to the home of Sayyidah 'Aaishah (radhiyallahu 'anha) and asked for some food. At that time,

Sayyidah 'Aaishah (radhiyallahu 'anha) was fasting, and besides a loaf of bread, she had no other food in her home.

Nevertheless, on seeing the beggar, she instructed her freed slave, "Give the bread to him." The freed slave responded, "There is nothing else for you to eat as iftaar (to break your fast)." However, Sayyidah 'Aaishah (radhiyallahu 'anha) insisted, "Give the bread to him." The freed slave thus obliged and gave the bread to the beggar.

That evening, a person who would not generally send food for Sayyidah 'Aaishah (radhiyallahu 'anha) unexpectedly sent her some goat meat covered in bread. On receiving the meat and bread, Sayyidah 'Aaishah (radhiyallahu 'anha) called her freed slave and said to her, "Eat this, for it is better than the bread that you wanted."

(Muwatta Imaam Maalik #3655)

Lessons:

❁ Sayyidah 'Aaishah (radhiyallahu 'anha) was not expecting this food to arrive, as it came from a person who was not in the habit of sending food for her. Hence, when she gave her bread to the beggar, she did so with complete reliance and trust in Allah Ta'ala to provide for her.

❁ When Allah Ta'ala sent food for her, He sent her food that was far better than that which she had given the beggar. Hence,

Sayyidah 'Aaishah (radhiyallahu 'anha) addressed her freed slave and taught her that when a person sacrifices something for the sake of Allah Ta'ala, then Allah Ta'ala will give him something far better in return.

❀ When we undergo financial constraints, we must constantly remind ourselves that it is Allah Ta'ala who provided for us till this point, and it is He alone that will provide for us in the future as well. The more we entrench this belief in our hearts and minds, the greater the peace of mind and calmness we will experience.

Passion for Spending on the Poor

As discussed, Sayyidah 'Aaishah (radhiyallahu 'anha) was extremely generous and loved spending on the poor. Hence, whenever she received any wealth, she would begin to spend it on the poor.

On one occasion, the dear and beloved nephew of Sayyidah 'Aaishah (radhiyallahu 'anha), Sayyiduna 'Abdullah bin Zubair (radhiyallahu 'anhuma), became concerned over the large amounts of wealth that she was spending in charity, and thus mentioned, "Her spending must be curtailed."

When Sayyidah 'Aaishah (radhiyallahu 'anha) heard about this, she was greatly disappointed that her nephew wished to restrict her in spending on the poor. In fact, her disappointment was so much that she took a vow to cease speaking to Sayyiduna 'Abdullah bin Zubair (radhiyallahu 'anhuma).

When Sayyiduna 'Abdullah bin Zubair (radhiyallahu 'anhuma) could not bear being separated and cut off from his beloved aunt for such a long time, he requested many people to intercede on his behalf. However, Sayyidah 'Aaishah (radhiyallahu 'anha) was not prepared to break her vow.

Eventually, when the separation became too much to bear, Sayyiduna 'Abdullah bin Zubair (radhiyallahu 'anhuma) approached Sayyiduna Miswar bin Makhramah (radhiyallahu 'anhu) and Sayyiduna 'Abdur Rahmaan bin Aswad (radhiyallahu 'anhu) asking them to intercede on his behalf and assist him to gain an audience with Sayyidah 'Aaishah (radhiyallahu 'anha). Sayyidah 'Aaishah (radhiyallahu 'anha) would show a lot of consideration to these Sahaabah (radhiyallahu 'anhum) on account of them being relatives of Rasulullah (sallallahu 'alaihi wasallam).

Accordingly, they went to the home of Sayyidah 'Aaishah (radhiyallahu 'anha) where Sayyiduna Miswar bin Makhramah (radhiyallahu 'anhu) and Sayyiduna 'Abdur Rahmaan bin Aswad (radhiyallahu 'anhu) asked permission to enter. Not knowing that Sayyiduna 'Abdullah bin Zubair (radhiyallahu 'anhuma) was with them, Sayyidah 'Aaishah (radhiyallahu 'anha) gave them all permission to enter.

They entered the home and remained behind the screen which separated them from her, while Sayyiduna 'Abdullah bin Zubair (radhiyallahu 'anhuma) seized the opportunity and went to the other side of the screen, hugging his aunt, weeping and begging her to forgive him. At the same time, Sayyiduna Miswar bin Makhramah (radhiyallahu 'anhu) and Sayyiduna 'Abdur Rahmaan bin Aswad (radhiyallahu 'anhu) interceded for Sayyiduna 'Abdullah (radhiyallahu 'anhu), urging Sayyidah 'Aaishah (radhiyallahu 'anha) to speak to him once again. Finally, Sayyidah 'Aaishah (radhiyallah 'anha) agreed and recommenced speaking to her nephew.

However, as compensation for breaking her vow, she thereafter freed forty slaves. **Furthermore, whenever she would think of the vow that she broke,** she would weep profusely, to the extent that her clothing would become wet with her tears, **as she had taken a vow in the name of Allah Ta'ala and thereafter broke the vow.**

(Saheeh Bukhaari #3503, #3505 & #6073 and Fat-hul Baari vol. 10, pg. 605)

Lessons:

Generally, when one person becomes upset with another person and ceases speaking to him, it is because he was insulted, offended, hurt or his ego was dented. In other words, it is generally due to a personal grievance and a trivial matter. However, in the case of Sayyidah 'Aaishah (radhiyallahu 'anha), her displeasure was for the sake of Deen, as she could not tolerate that her nephew wished to restrict the amount that she spent in charity.

❀ Sayyidah 'Aaishah (radhiyallahu 'anha) viewed breaking a vow that was made in the name of Allah Ta'ala as an extremely serious offence. Hence, instead of freeing one slave, which was the requirement, she 'went the extra mile' and freed forty slaves. Furthermore, due to her fear of accountability in the court of Allah Ta'ala, she continued expressing her regret and remorse by weeping profusely when recalling the incident.

❀ When Sayyiduna 'Abdullah bin Zubair (radhiyallahu 'anhuma) realised that he had made a mistake, he immediately tried his best to rectify it and repair the relationship with his aunt, even going to the extent of asking others to intercede for him and gain him an audience with her. In the same way, if we make a mistake or damage our relationship with some person, we should try our best to make amends and repair the damage.

❀ Sayyidah 'Aaishah (radhiyallahu 'anha) was blessed by Allah Ta'ala to be one of the blessed wives of Rasulullah (sallallahu 'alaihi wasallam). Hence, she was privileged to witness, first hand, the manner in which Rasulullah (sallallahu 'alaihi wasallam) conducted himself in the home, as well as other dimensions of the life of Rasulullah (sallallahu 'alaihi wasallam) which were not before the public. She thus possessed important knowledge of Deen which others required, due to which many people would come and learn Deen from her. However, when imparting this knowledge of Deen, she ensured that she remained behind a curtain where non-mahrams could not see her. Accordingly, in the incident above, it was only her nephew who went behind the curtain.

Selfless Consideration

When Sayyiduna 'Umar (radhiyallahu 'anhu) was stabbed whilst leading the Fajr Salaah, the wound proved to be fatal. Hence, his condition steadily deteriorated and his time in this world rapidly drew to an end.

During these final moments, he sent his son, Sayyiduna 'Abdullah bin 'Umar (radhiyallahu 'anhuma), to the home of Sayyidah 'Aaishah (radhiyallahu 'anha). Sayyiduna 'Umar (radhiyallahu 'anhu) instructed him thus, "Tell her that 'Umar conveys salaam. Do not tell her that Ameerul Mu-mineen conveys salaam, as today I am no longer Ameerul Mu-mineen (as I am about to pass away). After conveying salaam, tell her that 'Umar bin Khattaab requests permission to be buried alongside his companions, (Rasulullah [sallallahu 'alaihi wasallam] and Sayyiduna Abu Bakr [radhiyallahu 'anhu])."

The area in which they were buried formed part of the home of Sayyidah 'Aaishah (radhiyallahu 'anha). Hence, Sayyiduna 'Umar (radhiyallahu 'anhu) sought her permission to be buried there.

Following the instruction of his father, Sayyiduna 'Abdullah bin 'Umar (radhiyallahu 'anhuma) proceeded to the home of Sayyidah 'Aaishah (radhiyallahu 'anha) where he found her sitting and crying (over the loss that the Ummah would suffer through the demise of Sayyiduna 'Umar [radhiyallahu 'anhu]).

He conveyed the salaam of Sayyiduna 'Umar (radhiyallahu 'anhu) to her and then said, "'Umar requests permission to be buried with his companions." Hearing the request, Sayyidah 'Aaishah (radhiyallahu 'anha) mentioned, "I was hoping to be buried there myself. However, I will give preference today to 'Umar (radhiyallahu 'anhu) over myself."

When Sayyiduna 'Abdullah bin 'Umar (radhiyallahu 'anhuma) returned, and mentioned that Sayyidah 'Aaishah (radhiyallahu 'anha) had granted permission for him to be buried alongside Rasulullah (sallallahu 'alaihi wasallam) and Sayyiduna Abu Bakr (radhiyallahu 'anhu), Sayyiduna 'Umar (radhiyallahu 'anhu) further instructed his son saying, "After I pass away, carry my body (for the burial). Then repeat the request to Sayyidah 'Aaishah (radhiyallahu 'anha) by saying, ''Umar requests permission to be buried with his companions.' If she again grants permission, then bury me there. If not, then bury me in the cemetery of the Muslims."

Sometime later, Sayyidah 'Aaishah (radhiyallahu 'anha) mentioned that when it was just Rasulullah (sallallahu 'alaihi wasallam) and Sayyiduna Abu Bakr (radhiyallahu 'anhu) buried in the room, then when she would enter, she would not wear her outer garment, as it was her father and husband (sallallahu 'alaihi wasallam) buried there. However, after Sayyiduna 'Umar (radhiyallahu 'anhu) was buried in the room, she said, "By Allah! Whenever I thereafter entered the room, I wore my outer garment, out of hayaa (modesty) for 'Umar (radhiyallahu 'anhu)."

(Saheeh Bukhaari #3700 and Musnad Ahmad #25660)

Lessons:

❀ Who would not desire the good fortune of being buried alongside Rasulullah (sallallahu 'alaihi wasallam) and Sayyiduna Abu Bakr (radhiyallahu 'anhu)? However, despite this being his ardent desire, Sayyiduna 'Umar (radhiyallahu 'anhu) ensured that Sayyidah 'Aaishah (radhiyallahu 'anha) was not inconvenienced or oppressed in the process of fulfilling his wish. Hence, he insisted that the request be placed before Sayyidah 'Aaishah (radhiyallahu 'anha) for a second time, after his demise, in case she had a change of heart, or had initially found it difficult to refuse due to her respect for him.

❀ Although Sayyidah 'Aaishah (radhiyallahu 'anha) had the right to decline the request of Sayyiduna 'Umar (radhiyallahu 'anhu), especially as she herself wished to be buried in that area, she wholeheartedly sacrificed her own right and gave preference to Sayyiduna 'Umar (radhiyallahu 'anhu) over herself. This was no small sacrifice, as this piece of land is the most beloved in the sight of Allah Ta'ala! Hence, from this sacrifice, we can gauge the heart which she had, as well as the honour which she showed to Sayyiduna 'Umar (radhiyallahu 'anhu) as her senior. Conversely, we are sometimes so petty that we are not prepared to give the next person preference for even a trivial item, **and instead continuously complain as to why we are not given preferential treatment.**

❦   Sayyidah 'Aaishah (radhiyallahu 'anha) possessed such a high level of hayaa, and shamefulness was so embedded in her nature, that she even desisted from removing her outer garment before the grave of Sayyiduna 'Umar (radhiyallahu 'anhu)! When this was her level of hayaa before the grave of a non-mahram, we can well imagine the hayaa she displayed in regard to non-mahram men who were living.

Humble to the Last

When Sayyidah 'Aaishah (radhiyallahu 'anha) was lying on her deathbed, Sayyiduna 'Abdullah bin 'Abbaas (radhiyallahu 'anhuma) requested permission to enter, to which Sayyidah 'Aaishah (radhiyallahu 'anha) said, "I fear that he will praise me." Hearing this, her nephew, 'Abdullah bin 'Abdir Rahmaan (rahimahullah) felt that she did not wish to grant Sayyiduna 'Abdullah bin 'Abbaas (radhiyallahu 'anhuma) permission to enter, and thus interceded saying, "He is the cousin of Rasulullah (sallallahu 'alaihi wasallam) and from the seniors of the Muslims!" Sayyidah 'Aaishah (radhiyallahu 'anha) said, "Allow him to enter."

On entering, Sayyiduna 'Abdullah bin 'Abbaas (radhiyallahu 'anhuma) enquired as to how she was feeling, to which she replied, "I am well, provided I have taqwa." To this, Sayyiduna 'Abdullah bin 'Abbaas (radhiyallahu 'anhuma) responded, "In that case, you are well insha-Allah. The only thing that remains between you and meeting Rasulullah (sallallahu 'alaihi wasallam) and those whom you love (that have passed away) is for your soul to leave your body."

He then began to mention some of the virtues of Sayyidah 'Aaishah (radhiyallahu 'anha) saying, "You were the most beloved to Rasulullah (sallallahu 'alaihi wasallam) from all his wives, and Rasulullah (sallallahu 'alaihi wasallam) only loved that which was pure. He did not marry any virgin besides you. (When you were falsely accused of fornication,) your exoneration was revealed from the sky, through the medium of Jibreel ('alaihis salaam) and will be recited in every masjid on earth. When your necklace fell on the night of Abwaa, (and Rasulullah [sallallahu 'alaihi wasallam] halted the army to retrieve your necklace,) then the following morning, when Rasulullah (sallallahu 'alaihi wasallam) and the army of the Sahaabah (radhiyallahu 'anhum) had no water, Allah Ta'ala revealed the verse of tayammum. Thus, the concession of tayammum that Allah Ta'ala granted to this Ummah was on account of you. Therefore, by Allah, you are indeed blessed!"

When Sayyidah 'Aaishah (radhiyallahu 'anha) heard Sayyiduna 'Abdullah bin 'Abbaas (radhiyallahu 'anhuma) praising her in this manner, she said, "Please cease this, O Ibnu 'Abbaas! By the Being

Who controls my life, I wish that I was something totally forgotten!"

(Saheeh Bukhaari #4753, Musnad Ahmad #2496 and Fat-hul Baari)

Lessons:

🌹   Despite Sayyidah 'Aaishah (radhiyallahu 'anha) being blessed with all these outstanding virtues, she still thought nothing of herself. **Such was her level of humility that she did not wish to be praised, and even exclaimed, "I wish that I was something totally forgotten!"** In total contrast to this, we post every small detail of our lives on social media, merely to obtain the 'likes' and praises of others.

🌹   Sayyidah 'Aaishah (radhiyallahu 'anha) did not feel that she was deserving of Jannah due to her unique position. On the contrary, when Sayyidah 'Aaishah (radhiyallahu 'anha) was asked as to how she was, she replied that she was well – provided that **she possessed taqwa.** In other words, more than the family that one comes from, or who a person marries, it is the quality of taqwa that will pave the path to success.

Sayyidah Safiyyah (radhiyallahu 'anha)

Slavery over Freedom

Sayyidah Safiyyah (radhiyallahu 'anha) was the daughter of a Jewish leader, Huyayy bin Akhtab, who intensely hated and opposed Islam. He did his utmost to eradicate Deen and exterminate Rasulullah (sallallahu 'alaihi wasallam) and the Muslims. When Rasulullah (sallallahu 'alaihi wasallam) attacked Khaibar, Sayyidah Safiyyah (radhiyallahu 'anha) was among the prisoners that were captured.

Rasulullah (sallallahu 'alaihi wasallam) invited her to accept Islam, in which case he would keep her for himself. He (sallallahu 'alaihi wasallam) also allowed her to remain a Jew if she chose to do so, and even offered to free her, allowing her to reunite with her people.

However, her reply was, "O Rasulullah (sallallahu 'alaihi wasallam)! I have fallen in love with Islam and I have accepted you as the true Nabi of Allah. I do not have any desire to be a Jew. You have given me the option to choose between disbelief and Islam. Allah and His Rasul (sallallahu 'alaihi wasallam) are more beloved to me than freedom and returning to my people."

Hearing this reply of Sayyidah Safiyyah (radhiyallahu 'anha), Rasulullah (sallallahu 'alaihi wasallam) freed her and took her as his own respected wife.

(Saheeh Bukhaari #371 and Tabaqaat Ibni Sa'd vol. 8, pg. 123)

Lessons:

● Sayyidah Safiyyah (radhiyallahu 'anha) was given the choice between freedom with disbelief and slavery with Islam. Normally, a person would choose freedom over slavery. However, Allah Ta'ala and His Rasul (sallallahu 'alaihi wasallam) meant more to her than even freedom and returning to her own people. At times in life, we face a similar situation, where we have to choose between the 'restrictions' of Deen with the pleasure of Allah Ta'ala and the 'freedom' of the lifestyle of the disbelievers. As believers, we need to realize that the 'constraints' of Deen bring freedom in the Hereafter, whereas the 'freedom' of the lifestyle of the disbelievers brings misery in this world and the next. We thus need to choose Allah Ta'ala and His Rasul (sallallahu 'alaihi wasallam) over everything else.

● When a person makes a sacrifice and gives preference to the happiness of Allah Ta'ala and His Rasul (sallallahu 'alaihi wasallam), then apart from the rewards in the Hereafter, Allah

Ta'ala blesses the person in this world as well. Thus, in her situation, Allah Ta'ala blessed her with one of the greatest bounties that a woman can enjoy – becoming the respected wife of Rasulullah (sallallahu 'alaihi wasallam) and the mother of the believers!

Exemplary Respect

When Rasulullah (sallallahu 'alaihi wasallam) was departing from Khaibar, and his camel was brought, He (sallallahu 'alaihi wasallam) placed his blessed foot on the ground and knelt, offering Sayyidah Safiyyah (radhiyallahu 'anha) his thigh, so that she could place her foot on his thigh and mount the camel. However, she declined to place her foot on his blessed thigh, out of respect, and instead placed her knee on his blessed thigh in order to mount the camel.

Initially, some Sahaabah (radhiyallahu 'anhum), who did not witness the nikaah of Rasulullah (sallallahu 'alaihi wasallam) to Sayyidah Safiyyah (radhiyallahu 'anha), were not sure regarding whether Rasulullah (sallallahu 'alaihi wasallam) had kept Sayyidah Safiyyah (radhiyallahu 'anha) as his slave or had taken her as his respected wife. Due to the fact that hijaab and niqaab is necessary on free women, not on slave women, these Sahaabah (radhiyallahu 'anhum) said, "If he conceals her, she is his wife. If not, she is his slave."

When she mounted the camel, seated behind Rasulullah (sallallahu 'alaihi wasallam), he covered her body and face with his shawl, concealing her as he would conceal all his pure wives. Hence, these Sahaabah (radhiyallahu 'anhum) realized that she was the respected wife of Rasulullah (sallallahu 'alaihi wasallam) and not his slave girl.

(Tabaqaat Ibni Sa'd vol. 8, pg. 121 and Saheeh Muslim #3500)

Lessons:

❁ This incident highlights the consideration and compassion that Rasulullah (sallallahu 'alaihi wasallam) showed his respected wife as well as the exemplary respect that Sayyidah Safiyyah (radhiyallahu 'anha) displayed for Rasulullah (sallallahu 'alaihi wasallam). Although there was a need for her to step on the blessed thigh of Rasulullah (sallallahu 'alaihi wasallam) in order to mount the camel, especially due to her short stature, she did so without compromising her respect for Rasulullah (sallallahu 'alaihi wasallam). Respect (adab) is an integral part of our Deen, but it is unfortunately becoming extinct. A dedicated effort needs to be made to acquire this respect and instil it in our children.

❁ The statement of the Sahaabah (radhiyallahu 'anhum), "If he conceals her, she is his wife. If not, she is his slave," clearly shows that covering the body and the face is the hallmark of a free woman, whereas exposing the body, face, hair, etc. is the trademark of women who are enslaved. Hijaab and niqaab thus give a woman value and true freedom, whereas exposing herself cheapens her and enslaves her to the world around her.

Loyal to Islam

On one occasion, during the rule of Sayyiduna 'Umar (radhiyallahu 'anhu), a slave girl belonging to Sayyidah Safiyyah (radhiyallahu 'anha) came to him and complained that Sayyidah Safiyyah (radhiyallahu 'anha) loved the day of Saturday (the day of the Jews) and that she had ties with the Jews.

On receiving this information, which was serious, as a Muslim should honour the day of Friday and not have close ties with the disbelievers, Sayyiduna 'Umar (radhiyallahu 'anhu) called for Sayyidah Safiyyah (radhiyallahu 'anha) in order to investigate the information.

Sayyidah Safiyyah (radhiyallahu 'anha) explained that the accusation of her loving the day of Saturday was false, as since the day Allah Ta'ala had blessed her with the Day of Jumu'ah in place of Saturday (i.e. since she accepted Islam), she had no love for Saturday. As for her ties with the Jews, then they were her family, and she maintained these family ties (as maintaining ties is a basic teaching of Islam).

Sayyidah Safiyyah (radhiyallahu 'anha) then asked her slave girl what had caused her to carry these false allegations to

Sayyiduna 'Umar (radhiyallahu 'anhu). The slave girl replied, "Shaitaan." Thereafter, Sayyidah Safiyyah (radhiyallahu 'anha) freed her.

(Al-Istee'aab vol. 4, pg. 427)

Lessons:

❀ It is vital to verify information before acting on it or transmitting it to others, especially as there are many people who deliberately sow the seeds of misinformation in an effort to spread mischief and create fights, quarrels and disunity. Hence, failing to verify information leads to many misunderstandings and problems.

❀ For a Muslim, the greatest day of the week is the Day of Jumu'ah. A Muslim should love and honour this day more than any other day. Similarly, being Muslims, we should not show any love or honour to the special days and occasions of the disbelievers (e.g. Christmas, Easter, Diwali, New Years, etc.). We need to be proud of our Islamic culture, and not suffer from an inferiority complex.

❀ Maintaining family ties is so important that even if one's relatives are disbelievers, he should maintain ties with them, hoping to attract them to Islam. However, when doing so, one must ensure that he does not compromise in his Deen or allow his Deen to be affected.

❀ A Muslim will show kindness and good character to disbelievers, but will not become their friend and have love for them. When being friends and having love for the Jews and other disbelievers was such a serious matter for the Sahaabah (radhiyallahu 'anhum), that Sayyiduna 'Umar (radhiyallahu 'anhu) felt the need to investigate the matter, then would they have ever allowed us to emulate these disbelievers and mimic their every action, fashion and way?

❀ The highest level of good character is where a person is prepared to show good character to those who wrong and harm him. Sayyidah Safiyyah (radhiyallahu 'anha) displayed this high level of character by freeing the slave girl who had spread false rumours regarding her.

Unquestioning Submission

The Ansaar possessed such love for Rasulullah (sallallahu 'alaihi wasallam) and eagerness to be part of his blessed family that if any of them had a daughter of marriageable age, they would not get her married until they had first ascertained whether Rasulullah (sallallah 'alaihi wasallam) wished to marry her or not.

On one occasion, Rasulullah (sallallahu 'alaihi wasallam) approached an Ansaari Sahaabi and asked, "Please give me your daughter's hand in marriage." The Ansaari Sahaabi was overjoyed and exclaimed, "Certainly! It will be our honour, O Rasul of Allah (sallallahu 'alaihi wasallam), and our pleasure!" Rasulullah (sallallahu 'alaihi wasallam) then said, "However, I am not requesting her hand for myself." The Sahaabi asked, "Then on whose behalf are you proposing, O Rasul of Allah (sallallahu 'alaihi wasallam)?" Rasulullah (sallallahu 'alaihi wasallam) responded, "On behalf of Julaibeeb." Hearing this, the Sahaabi requested, "O Rasul of Allah (sallallahu 'alaihi wasallam)! Let me check with her mother."

The Sahaabi then went to his wife and said, "The Rasul of Allah (sallallahu 'alaihi wasallam) has asked for your daughter's hand in marriage." His wife responded, "Yes, and it will be my pleasure!" The Sahaabi then said, "Rasulullah (sallallahu 'alaihi wasallam) is not asking for her hand for himself. Rather, he is proposing on behalf of Julaibeeb."

When the mother heard this, she exclaimed, "What! Julaibeeb? Never! We will not get our daughter married to him! Did Rasulullah (sallallahu 'alaihi wasallam) not find someone better than Julaibeeb? We turned down far better proposals than Julaibeeb for our daughter!"

The reason for her responding in this manner was that Sayyiduna Julaibeeb (radhiyallahu 'anhu) was short in stature and dark in complexion.

Thereafter, as the Sahaabi stood to leave the home and give their response to Rasulullah (sallallahu 'alaihi wasallam), his daughter, who was listening from behind the curtain, asked, "Who sent the proposal for me?" When her mother informed her that the proposal had been sent by Rasulullah (sallallahu 'alaihi wasallam) himself, she said, "Are you rejecting the instruction of Rasulullah (sallallahu 'alaihi wasallam)? If Rasulullah (sallallahu 'alaihi wasalam) is pleased with him (as my husband), marry me to him, as it will never lead to my ruin!"

When the young girl spoke these words, her parents realized that she was right and said to her, "You have spoken the truth." Her father thus returned to Rasulullah (sallallahu 'alaihi wasallam) and said, "If you are pleased with Julaibeeb (marrying our daughter), then we are also pleased with him." Rasulullah (sallallahu 'alahi wasallam) responded, "I am indeed pleased with him." Rasulullah (sallallahu 'alaihi wasallam) then performed her nikaah to Sayyiduna Julaibeeb (radhiyallahu 'anhu), and made a special du'aa for her saying, "O Allah! Shower immense goodness upon her, and do not make her life constrained and difficult!"

Sometime thereafter, Rasulullah (sallallahu 'alauihi wasallam) and the Sahaabah (radhiyallahu 'anhum) went out in jihaad, and Allah Ta'ala blessed them with victory. After the battle was concluded, Rasulullah (sallallahu 'alaihi wasallam) began to search for the Sahaabah (radhiyallahu 'anhum) who had fallen and gained martyrdom. Rasulullah (sallallahu 'alaihi wasallam) asked the Sahaabah (radhiyallahu 'anhum), "Is there anyone missing (i.e. fallen as a martyr)?" The Sahaabah (radhiyallahu 'anhum) answered in the affirmative, and named a few individuals. Rasulullah (sallallahu 'alaihi wasallam) then repeated the question, and they again named a few individuals.

When Rasulullah (sallallahu 'alaihi wasallam) enquired for the third time, the Sahaabah (radhiyallahu 'anhum) replied that they were unaware of anyone else missing. Rasulullah (sallallahu 'alaihi wasallam) then said, "However, I cannot see Julaibeeb. Search for him among the fallen." The Sahaabah (radhiyallahu 'anhum) thus searched, and on locating his body, they said to Rasulullah (sallallahu 'alaihi wasallam), "O Rasul of Allah (sallallahu 'alaihi wasallam)! Here he is, beside the body of seven disbelievers whom he killed before he succumbed to their blows and died."

Rasulullah (sallallahu 'alaihi wasallam) stood over the body of Sayyiduna Julaibeeb (radhiyallahu 'anhu) and said, "He killed seven disbelievers before they managed to kill him!" **Out of extreme happiness with the heroism, bravery and sacrifice of Julaibeeb (radhiyallahu 'anhu),** Rasulullah (sallallahu 'alaihi wasallam) said twice or thrice, "He is from me and I am from him!"

The Sahaabah (radhiyallahu 'anhum) thereafter dug a grave for him. While the grave was being dug, instead of placing the body of Sayyiduna Julaibeeb (radhiyallahu 'anhu) on a bier, Rasulullah (sallallahu 'alaihi wasallam) carried it in his own blessed arms and thereafter placed it in the grave.

As far as his wife is concerned, then it is reported that on account of the special du'aa that Rasulullah (sallallahu 'alaihi wasallam) had made for her, there was no widow, among the Ansaar, who was more highly sought after (or more prosperous) than her.

(Musnad Ahmad #12393 & #19784)

Lessons:

❀ The young girl of the Ansaar understood that if Rasulullah (sallallahu 'alaihi wasalam) had recommended something for her, then it must certainly and definitely be in her best interest. Hence, even though the recommendation did not outwardly appear attractive, she ensured that she accepted it. This should be the mindset of every believer – he should understand that the way of Rasulullah (sallallahu 'alaihi wasallam) is not only the best way for him, it is the only way for him. If one does so, one will secure the immense blessings of the sunnah and will secure the pleasure of Rasulullah (sallallahu 'alaihi wasallam), just as this Sahaabiyyah (radhiyallahu 'anha) acquired the special du'aa of Rasulullah (sallallahu 'alaihi wasallam) due to which she enjoyed a respectful and comfortable life.

❀   There is no harm in one marrying an attractive spouse. However, more important than the external appearance of the spouse is their character and commitment to Deen. **In the absence of these qualities, the husband may destroy his wife's worldly life (by oppressing her) and even worse – her Jannah (by leading her into sin).**

Allah before Emotions

Sayyidah Asmaa (radhiyallahu 'anha) was the daughter of Sayyiduna Abu Bakr Siddeeq (radhiyallahu 'anhu) and the half-sister of Sayyidah 'Aaishah (radhiyallahu 'anha). Sayyiduna Abu Bakr (radhiyallahu 'anhu) had divorced the mother of Sayyidah Asmaa (radhiyallahu 'anha) during the pre-Islamic era, thereafter marrying Sayyidah Ummu Rumaan (radhiyallahu 'anha) who later bore him Sayyidah 'Aaishah (radhiyallahu 'anha).

During the period of the treaty of Hudaibiyah, the mother of Sayyidah Asmaa (radhiyallahu 'anha) came to Madeenah Munawwarah accompanied by her son, Haarith. Her name was Qutailah, and she had not accepted Islam. On arriving in Madeenah Munawwarah, she wished to visit her daughter, Sayyidah Asmaa (radhiyallahu 'anha). She had brought gifts for her, and also wished to seek financial assistance from Sayyidah Asmaa (radhiyallahu 'anha).

As soon as Sayyidah Asmaa (radhiyallahu 'anha) saw that her mother had come to visit, she refused to accept her gifts and did not allow her into her home, as she had not accepted Islam – even though it had been more than six years since she had last met her mother!

Instead, she sent a message to her half-sister, Sayyidah 'Aaishah (radhiyallahu 'anhu), requesting her to convey the following question to Rasulullah (sallallahu 'alaihi wasallam), "My mother has come to visit me, and she also wishes for some financial assistance from me. What should I do? Should I maintain my relationship with her?" Rasulullah (sallallahu 'alaihi wasallam) replied, "Yes, she should maintain her relationship with her mother. She should allow her into her home and she should accept the gifts as well."

Only after securing the permission of Rasulullah (sallallahu 'alaihi wasallam) did Sayyidah Asmaa (radhiyallahu 'anha) allow her mother into her home, show her kindness and accept her gifts.

(Saheeh Bukhaari #2620, Fat-hul Baari and Tabaqaat Ibni Sa'd vol. 8, pg. 252)

Lessons:

The primary concern of the Sahaabah (radhiyallahu 'anhum) was securing the happiness of Allah Ta'ala. Due to the mother of Sayyidah Asmaa (radhiyallahu 'anha) not being a Muslim, she was unsure whether it was permissible or not for her to accept her gifts and allow her into the home. Hence, to ensure that she did not disobey Allah Ta'ala, she immediately acquired guidance from Rasulullah (sallallahu 'alaihi wasallam). Similarly, we should ensure that we remain linked to the pious 'Ulama (keeping within the parameters of sharee'ah) so that we can seek guidance in all branches of life, thus always remaining in the happiness of Allah Ta'ala.

❁ The demand of imaan is that we put Allah Ta'ala and Deen before our emotions. Sayyidah Asmaa (radhiyallahu 'anha) was obviously affected by the sight of her mother, especially after such a long period of separation. However, she put her emotions aside and first ensured that she was pleasing Allah Ta'ala. The Sahaabah (radhiyallahu 'anhum) valued their relationship with Allah Ta'ala more than their relationship with their own parents, children, etc.

Modesty – No Matter What!

During the Battle of the Trench, the Banu Quraizah, a clan of Jews near Madeenah Munawwarah, broke their peace treaty with the Muslims. At this crucial juncture, they decided to oppose the Muslims and side with their enemy, the Quraish. After the Quraish returned to Makkah Mukarramah without victory, Rasulullah (sallallahu 'alaihi wasallam) was commanded by Allah Ta'ala to march on the Banu Quraizah due to their betrayal and treachery.

It was during this expedition against the Banu Quraizah that a Jewess named Bunaanah flung a rock from a hilltop, striking Sayyiduna Khallaad bin Suwaid (radhiyallahu 'anhu) and causing his martyrdom.

On their return to Madeenah Munawwarah, the mother of this Sahaabi, Sayyidah Ummu Khallaad (radhiyallahu 'anha), came to Rasulullah (sallallahu 'alaihi wasallam) to enquire regarding her son's reward and status in the Hereafter. However, despite the tragedy of just losing her beloved son, she was not unmindful of her modesty and thus ensured that she kept her niqaab (purdah) on, concealing her face. **Noticing her commitment to niqaab, even** in these moments, a Sahaabi exclaimed, "You have come to enquire about your son (who was martyred) yet you have still covered your face (in this tragic moment)?" She replied, "I may have lost my son, but I have not lost my hayaa (modesty)."

(Sunan Abi Dawood #2488, Bazlul Majhood vol. 4, pg. 197 and Tabaqaat Ibni Sa'd vol. 3, pg. 530)

Lesson:

❀ The words of Sayyidah Ummu Khallaad (radhiyallahu 'anha) are indeed worthy of being engraved into the heart of every Muslim. The essence of her response was that no matter where she was, or what happened to her, she would not, under any condition, lose her hayaa (modesty), as her hayaa was an inseparable part of her identity.

The Supportive Spouse

Sayyidah Zainab Thaqafiyyah (radhiyallahu 'anha), also known by the name 'Raitah', was the respected wife of the renowned Sahaabi, Sayyiduna 'Abdullah bin Mas'ood (radhiyallahu 'anhu).

Sayyiduna 'Abdullah bin Mas'ood (radhiyallahu 'anhu) had dedicated his time to remaining in the blessed company of Rasulullah (sallallahu 'alaihi wasallam) serving him and acquiring the knowledge of Deen from him. Through this effort, Allah Ta'ala blessed him to become one of the leading Sahaabah (radhiyallahu 'anhum) in the field of the knowledge of Deen.

Sayyiduna 'Abdullah bin Mas'ood (radhiyallahu 'anhu) did not possess abundant wealth, and had sacrificed earning a living to acquire the knowledge of Deen from Rasulullah (sallallahu 'alaihi wasallam). His wife, Sayyidah Zainab (radhiyallahu 'anha), not only accepted his decision happily, but even tried her best to assist him in this noble endeavour! She would thus see to the needs of the household – which included the orphaned children of her brother and sister – by making and selling things (from home) to earn an income.

One day, Sayyidah Zainab (radhiyallahu 'anha) heard Rasulullah (sallallahu 'alaihi wasallam) address the women saying, "Give charity, even if it be through selling your jewellery!" When she heard this, Sayyidah Zainab (radhiyallahu 'anha) mentioned to Sayyiduna 'Abdullah bin Mas'ood (radhiyallahu 'anhu), "By spending on the household, I am unable to give money in charity!" Sayyiduna 'Abdullah bin Mas'ood (radhiyallahu 'anhu) answered, "If spending on your household is not rewarding for you, I would not be happy for you to spend on us."

Sayyidah Zainab (radhiyallahu 'anha) thus went to Rasulullah (sallallahu 'alaihi wasallam) and expressed her concern to him saying, "I am a woman who makes things and sells (from home). Neither my husband, my children nor I possess wealth. Due to spending on my family, I am unable to give money in charity. Will I receive the reward of charity for spending on them?" Rasulullah (sallallahu 'alaihi wasallam) replied, "So long as you spend on them, you will receive the reward of charity, so continue spending on them." In another narration, Rasulullah (sallallahu 'alaihi wasallam) said that she would receive a double reward; one for maintaining family ties (through spending on family) and a separate reward for charity.

(Saheeh Bukhaari #1466, Fat-hul Baari and Usdul Ghaabah vol. 5, pgs. 291 & 302)

Lessons:

❀   When a woman assists her husband and children in their Deeni endeavours, then even though she may be comfortable in her home while they are out doing Deeni work, she has a full share in their efforts and thus shares in their rewards as well. Hence, Sayyidah Zainab (radhiyallahu 'anha) was not only running a 'home industry', she was running a full-blown factory that was generating rewards in the Aakhirah on an industrial scale.

❀ When giving charity, a person should first try to find recipients from his own family, as he will earn a double reward by giving to relatives. When helping family members, he should not embarrass them by saying that it is charity, but should rather give it in the guise of a gift. However, although charity begins at home, it does not end there. If a person has surplus money to give in charity, he should also give to other recipients and spend in other avenues as well.

❀ Although they did not have abundant wealth, Sayyidah Zainab (radhiyallahu 'anha) had taken in her brother's and sister's orphaned children, raising them while spending from her own money. This is the spirit advocated by Islam – the spirit of love, compassion, sympathy, generosity and caring for one and all.

❀ Despite the good deeds that she was already performing, Sayyidah Zainab (radhiyallahu 'anha) was not complacent. Rather, she wanted to increase her good deeds by giving charity as well, even though she did not possess abundant wealth.

Glimpses of True Love

The Day of Uhud was indeed a severe day for the Muslims, as no less than seventy Sahaabah (radhiyallahu 'anhum) were martyred in the battle against the disbelievers.

In the aftermath of the battle, a few women of Madeenah Munawwarah made their way to Uhud to enquire after their near and dear ones. Among them was Sayyidah 'Aaishah (radhiyallahu 'anha).

En-route, she encountered Sayyidah Hind bintu 'Amr bin Haraam (radhiyallahu 'anha) who was driving a camel which carried the bodies of three martyrs on it. Sayyidah 'Aaishah (radhiyallahu 'anha) asked her regarding the condition of the Muslims in Uhud. Sayyidah Hind (radhiyallahu 'anha) replied, "(They are in a) good (state). As for Rasulullah (sallallahu 'alaihi wasallam), he is safe, and every calamity is easy to bear after him (i.e. after knowing that he [sallallahu 'alaihi wasallam] is safe)! As for the other Muslims, then Allah Ta'ala blessed some of them with martyrdom, and He turned back the disbelievers with their fury (rage), not having acquired any good. And Allah Ta'ala was sufficient for the believers in battle, and Allah Ta'ala is Most Powerful and Most Mighty."

Sayyidah 'Aaishah (radhiyallahu 'anha) then gestured towards the bodies on the camel and asked her, "Who are these (martyrs)?" She replied, "My brother (Sayyiduna 'Abdullah bin 'Amr bin Haraam [radhiyallahu 'anhu]), my son, Khallaad (radhiyallahu 'anhu), and my husband, 'Amr bin Jamooh (radhiyallahu 'anhu)."

Sayyidah 'Aaishah (radhiyallahu 'anha) asked her, "Where are you taking their bodies?" She replied, "I am taking them to Madeenah Munawwarah to be buried there." Saying this, she urged the camel to move, but the camel refused to move towards Madeenah Munawwarah and instead knelt on its knees. Observing this, Sayyidah 'Aaishah (radhiyallahu 'anha) commented, "The camel is perhaps kneeling as it cannot manage carrying a load this heavy?" Sayyidah Hind (radhiyallahu 'anha) responded, "That is not the problem! This camel often carried the load of two camels! I suspect that there is some other reason for it kneeling." She then reprimanded the camel, succeeding in making it stand, but when she directed it towards Madeenah Munawwarah, it knelt once again and refused to move.

Eventually, when she turned the camel back towards Uhud, the camel proceeded swiftly. On returning to Uhud, she went to Rasulullah (sallallahu 'alaihi wasallam) and informed him of the camel's refusal to take the bodies to Madeenah Munawwarah. On hearing this, Rasulullah (sallallahu 'alaihi wasallam) replied, "This camel has been commanded (by Allah Ta'ala). Did 'Amr (radhiyallahu 'anhu) say anything (before leaving for Uhud)?" Sayyidah Hind (radhiyallahu 'anha) replied, "When he was heading towards Uhud, he faced the qiblah and made du'aa saying, "O Allah! Do not send me back to my family as a failure, and bless me with martyrdom!"

Hearing this, Rasulullah (sallallahu 'alaihi wasallam) said, "That is the reason why the camel is refusing to move (towards Madeenah Munawwarah, as 'Amr [radhiyallahu 'anhu] had made du'aa that he should not return home)." Rasulullah (sallallahu 'alaihi wasallam) then said, "From you, O Ansaar, there are certain people who are such (i.e. so beloved to Allah Ta'ala) that if he takes an oath in the name of Allah Ta'ala, then Allah Ta'ala will most certainly fulfill his oath, and one such person is 'Amr bin Jamooh (radhiyallahu 'anhu). I have indeed seen him walking with his limp in Jannah. O Hind! The angels have continued to shade your brother, from the time he was killed until now, waiting for him to be buried."

After they were buried, Rasulullah (sallallahu 'alaihi wasallam) addressed Sayyidah Hind (radhiyallahu 'anha) and said, "O Hind! All of them are together in Jannah." She replied, "O Rasul of Allah (sallallahu 'alaihi wasallam)! Make du'aa to Allah Ta'ala to allow me to be with them!"

(Al-Maghaazi - Waaqidi vol. 1, pg. 265 and Subulul Hudaa war Rashaad vol. 4, pg. 214)

Similar to the incident of Sayyidah Hind (radhiyallahu 'anha) is the incident of another Ansaari woman, from the Banu Dinaar clan, who also came to Uhud to enquire after her near and dear ones. As she proceeded through Uhud, she passed by the bodies of her father, son, husband and brother, all of whom achieved martyrdom. As she passed each body, she asked, "Who is this?" and at each body, she was told in turn, "Your father", "Your brother", "Your husband" and "Your son".

Despite these being her closest family members, she did not pause at any of the bodies, but continued ahead asking, "How is the Rasul of Allah (sallallahu 'alaihi wasallam)?" The Sahaabah (radhiyallahu 'anhum) replied, "By the grace of Allah Ta'ala, he is as you would like (i.e. he is safe and sound)." However, she was not satisfied, and said, "Show him to me so that I may see him (i.e. I may see with my own eyes that he is indeed safe)." They told her that Rasulullah (sallallahu 'alaihi wasallam) was ahead and pointed towards him.

When she found Rasulullah (sallallahu 'alaihi wasallam), she held onto the corner of his blessed clothing and exclaimed, "May my father and mother be sacrificed for you, O Rasul of Allah (sallallahu 'alaihi wasallam)! Every calamity is easy to bear and not a matter of concern, after knowing that you are safe from any harm!"

(Tabraani - Majma'uz Zawaaid #10145 and Seerah Ibni Hishaam vol. 3, pg. 99)

Lessons:

 The Sahaabah (radhiyallahu 'anhum) had such love for Rasulullah (sallallahu 'alaihi wasallam), that it surpassed their love for their own kith and kin and even their ownselves. There are other similar incidents recorded of other women who had lost their family members in the Battle of Uhud, yet expressed that their greater concern was for the safety of Rasulullah (sallallahu 'alaihi wasallam). It was this love for Rasulullah (sallallahu 'alaihi wasallam) that motivated them to follow his every guidance, teaching and command unquestioningly and display complete submission before him. Hence, the mark of true love for Rasulullah (sallallahu 'alaihi wasallam) is that one sacrifices his own ways, ideas, inclinations and mindset for that of Rasulullah (sallallahu 'alaihi wasallam) and the sunnah.

❀ In the path of Deen, there was no sacrifice too great for the Sahaabah (radhiyallahu 'anhum). They were prepared to sacrifice their wealth, parents and even their children in the path of Allah Ta'ala. At the very least, we should sacrifice our impermissible desires and unlawful demands of our family members to remain loyal to Allah Ta'ala and earn His pleasure.

Absolute Submission

Sayyiduna Mugheerah bin Shu'bah (radhiyallahu 'anhu) reports the following incident:

On one occasion, I sent a marriage proposal to a girl of the Ansaar. When I mentioned this to Rasulullah (sallallahu 'alaihi wasallam), he asked me, "Did you see the girl?" I replied in the negative. Rasulullah (sallallahu 'alaihi wasallam) then recommended to me, "Look at her, for it is more likely that there will be affection and love between you (i.e. if you marry her after looking at her and finding her pleasing to your eye, there will be a greater chance of your marriage prospering)."

I thus proceeded to the girl's home and told her parents what Rasulullah (sallallahu 'alaihi wasallam) had advised. They were however reluctant, and therefore, I stood up to leave.

As I was leaving, the girl asked her parents to call me back. When I returned, she stood at the edge of the curtain and said, "If Rasulullah (sallallahu 'alaihi wasallam) instructed you to look at me then I permit you to do so; if not, then I strictly forbid you to look at me." Accordingly, I looked at her and married her. Subsequently, she was extremely beloved to me and honoured in my sight.

(Ibnun Najjaar - Kanzul 'Ummaal #45619)

Lessons:

❁ The hayaa (modesty) of the Sahaabah (radhiyallahu 'anhum) and their protectiveness over their womenfolk was such that the parents of the girl were initially reluctant when Sayyiduna Mugheerah (radhiyallahu 'anhu) requested to see their daughter. Similarly, until she learnt that it was the instruction of Rasulullah (sallallahu 'alaihi wasallam), the daughter was not prepared to allow any strange man to look at her.

❁ The Sahaabah (radhiyallahu 'anhum) were blessed with the quality of absolute submission before the instruction of Rasulullah (sallallahu 'alaihi wasallam). Hence, they always put their own intellect, understanding and emotions aside and fully complied with the wishes and desires of Rasulullah (sallallahu 'alaihi wasallam). They understood that this was the key to success in both the worlds. Similarly, if we desire true happiness and success, we will have to adhere strictly to the teachings of Deen.

❁ Rasulullah (sallallahu 'alaihi wasallam) has taught us the guidelines that need to be adhered to regarding marriage, and has told us that following these guidelines are the key to a prosperous marriage. Hence, if we surpass the bounds of sharee'ah and begin to engage in impermissible practices, such as the boy and girl communicating or even dating before marriage, we will lose the barakah (blessings) and help of Allah Ta'ala which is essential for the marriage to prosper. Thus, we should always refer to the

'Ulama to find out the limits of sharee'ah so that we can ensure that we remain within the parameters of Deen.

Sayyidah Asmaa bintu 'Umais (radhiyallahu 'anha)

Blessed with the Best

Every woman would love to be married to the 'dream' husband. In this regard, there was one Sahaabiyyah who was privileged to have been in the nikaah of not one, but three of the best husbands of this Ummah (two of whom were from the four Khulafaa). This was none other than Sayyidah Asmaa bintu 'Umais (radhiyallahu 'anha).

She was initially married to Sayyiduna Ja'far bin Abi Taalib (radhiyallahu 'anhu), the cousin of Rasulullah (sallallahu 'alaihi wasallam) and elder brother of Sayyiduna 'Ali (radhiyallahu 'anhu) by ten years. She bore him three sons viz. 'Abdullah, Muhammad and 'Awn (radhiyallahu 'anhum). She remained in his nikaah until she was widowed with his martyrdom in the Battle of Mutah.

Thereafter, on the occasion of the Battle of Hunain, Rasulullah (sallallahu 'alaihi wasallam) himself performed her nikaah to

Sayyiduna Abu Bakr (radhiyallahu 'anhu). While married to Sayyiduna Abu Bakr (radhiyallahu 'anhu), she gave birth to his son, Muhammad (radhiyallahu 'anhu), en-route to hajj during the final hajj of Rasulullah (sallallahu 'alaihi wasallam).

After Sayyiduna Abu Bakr (radhiyallahu 'anhu) departed from this world, she was blessed with the good fortune of entering into the nikaah of Sayyiduna 'Ali (radhiyallahu 'anhu). She bore him two sons, Yahya and 'Awn (rahimahumallah).

Apart from having the best of husbands, she also had the best of sisters. Her sisters were Sayyidah Maimoonah (radhiyallahu 'anha), the respected wife of Rasulullah (sallallahu 'alaihi wasallam), Sayyidah Ummul Fadhl (radhiyallahu 'anha), the respected wife of Sayyiduna 'Abbaas (radhiyallahu 'anhu), and Sayyidah Salma bintul Haarith (radhiyallahu 'anha), the respected wife of Sayyiduna Hamzah (radhiyallahu 'anhu).

Sayyidah Asmaa bintu 'Umais (radhiyallahu 'anha) had brought imaan during the initial period of Islam, before the Sahaabah (radhiyallahu 'anhum) began to congregate in Daarul Arqam (the home of Sayyiduna Arqam [radhiyallahu 'anhu]). She had pledged allegiance to Rasulullah (sallallahu 'alaihi wasallam), and when permission was granted to the Sahaabah (radhiyallahu 'anhum) to migrate to Abyssinia, she and her husband migrated to escape the persecution of the Quraish.

They returned from Abyssinia to Madeenah Munawwarah on the occasion of the conquest of Khaibar. Rasulullah (sallallahu 'alaihi wasallam) was so pleased at their return that he kissed

Sayyiduna Ja'far (radhiyallahu 'anhu) between his eyes and said, "I do not know which is more pleasing to me, the return of Ja'far (radhiyallahu 'anhu) or the conquest of Khaibar." It was just a few months after their return from Abyssinia that Sayyiduna Ja'far (radhiyallahu 'anhu) was blessed with martyrdom at Mutah.

Sayyidah Asmaa bintu 'Umais (radhiyallahu 'anha) passed away in the year 38 A.H.

(*Siyaru Aa'laamin Nubalaa* vol. 1, pg. 206 & vol. 2, pg. 283, *Usdul Ghaabah* vol. 5, pg. 213, *Al-Isaabah* vol. 8, pg. 15, *Saheeh Muslim* #2950, *Mustadrak Haakim* #6801 & #4941 and *Al-Bidaayah wan Nihaayah* vol. 8, pg. 107)

There are numerous unique and inspirational incidents that transpired in the life of this illustrious Sahaabiyyah, some of which are discussed below.

Competing in Kindness and Care

On the occasion of the 'Umratul Qadhaa (the qadhaa 'Umrah performed by Rasulullah [sallallahu 'alaihi wasallam] and the Sahaabah [radhiyallahu 'anhum] after the Treaty of Hudaibiyah, in the following year), the disbelievers allowed Rasulullah (sallallahu 'alaihi wasallam) and the Sahaabah (radhiyallahu 'anhum) to remain in Makkah Mukarramah for just three days, after which they had to depart.

As they were departing from Makkah Mukarramah, the orphaned daughter of Sayyiduna Hamzah (radhiyallahu 'anhu), Sayyidah 'Umaarah (radhiyallahu 'anha), came behind Rasulullah (sallallahu 'alaihi wasallam) calling out, "O my uncle! O my uncle!" She had been living in Makkah Mukarramah until then but now wished to leave Makkah Mukarramah and join the Muslims in Madeenah Munawwarah. Seeing her, Sayyiduna 'Ali (radhiyallahu 'anhu) made her over to Sayyidah Faatimah (radhiyallahu 'anha), who was seated in her carriage atop the camel, and said to her, "Here is your cousin, take her!" Sayyiduna 'Ali (radhiyallahu 'anhu) was unhappy for her to remain among the disbelievers in Makkah Mukarramah.

According to some narrations, it was Sayyiduna Zaid bin Haarithah (radhiyallahu 'anhu) who had encouraged the daughter of Sayyiduna Hamzah (radhiyallahu 'anhu) to leave Makkah Mukarramah and join the Muslims.

After arriving in Madeenah Munawwarah, Sayyiduna 'Ali (radhiyallahu 'anhu), Sayyiduna Zaid (radhiyallahu 'anhu) and Sayyiduna Ja'far bin Abi Taalib (radhiyallahu 'anhu) all began to debate as to who would have the privilege of taking the daughter of Sayyiduna Hamzah (radhiyallahu 'anhu) into his home to care for her.

Sayyiduna 'Ali (radhiyallahu 'anhu) explained, "I am the one who took her (when we left Makkah Mukarramah), she is the daughter of my uncle, and I am married to the daughter of Rasulullah (sallallahu 'alaihi wasallam) who is most rightful of looking after her."

Sayyiduna Ja'far (radhiyallahu 'anhu) then said, "I am the most rightful to look after her as she is the daughter of my uncle, and I am also married to her maternal aunt (referring to Sayyidah Asmaa bintu 'Umais [radhiyallahu 'anha])."

Finally, Sayyiduna Zaid (radhiyallahu 'anhu) said, "I am the most rightful one to look after her as she is the daughter of my brother (as Rasulullah [sallallahu 'alaihi wasallam] had formed the pact of 'muaakhaat' [brotherhood] between Sayyiduna Hamzah [radhiyallahu 'anhu] and myself)."

After hearing the motivation of all three Sahaabah (radhiyallahu 'anhum), Rasulullah (sallallahu 'alaihi wasallam) passed the decision that the daughter of Sayyiduna Hamzah (radhiyallahu 'anhu) would be in the care of Sayyiduna Ja'far (radhiyallahu 'anhu), as his wife was the maternal aunt of the orphaned girl. Rasulullah (sallallahu 'alaihi wasallam) explained saying, "The maternal aunt is like the mother."

Then, in order to please the heart of Sayyiduna 'Ali (radhiyallahu 'anhu), Rasulullah (sallallahu 'alaihi wasallam) said to him, "You are from me and I am from you (i.e. we are from the same family, you are married to my daughter and we share a special bond of love)."

Similarly, to please the heart of Sayyiduna Ja'far (radhiyallahu 'anhu), Rasulullah (sallallahu 'alaihi wasallam) said to him, "You resemble me in physical appearance as well as in character."

Finally, to please the heart of Sayyiduna Zaid (radhiyallahu 'anhu), Rasulullah (sallallahu 'alaihi wasallam) said to him, "You are our brother (in imaan) and our freed slave."

In this manner, she remained in the care of Sayyidah Asmaa bintu 'Umais (radhiyallahu 'anha) and Sayyiduna Ja'far (radhiyallahu 'anhu) until he was martyred. Thereafter, it was Sayyiduna 'Ali (radhiyallahu 'anhu) who took her into his care.

(Saheeh Bukhaari #4251 and Fat-hul Baari)

Lessons:

Sayyidah Asmaa bintu 'Umais (radhiyallahu 'anha) was not only prepared to take her niece into her home, but she and her husband 'fought' for the privilege to do so. **In fact, from the conduct of all three Sahaabah (radhiyallahu 'anhum), we can clearly see the value of kindness and sympathy which dominated their blessed hearts.** Hence, they did not consider this young orphaned girl a burden, but rather considered it an honour and privilege to take her into their homes. **Without such values, although our homes may be huge, our hearts will be small,** due to which we will not even be prepared to keep our own parents in our homes (Allah Ta'ala forbid!).

❀ The concern of Sayyiduna 'Ali (radhiyallahu 'anhu) was that this young, Muslim girl should not remain in Makkah Mukarramah in the midst of the disbelievers. Hence, he wished to take her to Madeenah Munawwarah where she would have a Muslim family structure to support her as well as an Islamic environment in which to live. If this was their worry, then imagine how much more concern we should have for our children, especially when sending them to other cities, or even countries, to study, where they will be unsupervised by family, and will be left completely exposed to the influences of the environment for an extended period of time!

❀ Such was the blessed character of Rasulullah (sallallahu 'alaihi wasallam) that even when he passed the decision in favour of one Sahaabi, he comforted the hearts of all the Sahaabah (radhiyallahu 'anhum) by telling them such things that brought delight to their hearts. In essence, Rasulullah (sallallahu 'alaihi wasallam) always tried to bring happiness to the hearts of the Sahaabah (radhiyallahu 'anhum) and avoided causing pain to anyone.

Happiness in Deeni Progress

Sayyidah Asmaa bintu 'Umais (radhiyallahu 'anha) and her husband, Sayyiduna Ja'far (radhiyallahu 'anhu), had performed hijrah (migration) to Abyssinia together with some other Sahaabah (radhiyallahu 'anhum) to escape the persecution of the Quraish. Hence, they lived in Abyssinia, far from their homeland, until Rasulullah (sallallahu 'alaihi wasallam) sent Sayyiduna 'Amr bin Umayyah (radhiyallahu 'anhu) to the King of Abyssinia, requesting him to send Sayyiduna Ja'far (radhiyallahu 'anhu) and his companions back to Arabia to join Rasulullah (sallallahu 'alaihi wasallam).

They thus set off by ship and met Rasulullah (sallallahu 'alaihi wasallam) just after the Muslims conquered Khaibar. However, as they had migrated to Madeenah Munawwarah so late (approximately six or seven years after the hijrah of Rasulullah [sallallahu 'alaihi wasallam]), many people would say to them, "We preceded you in performing hijrah."

One day, while Sayyidah Asmaa (radhiyallahu 'anha) was visiting Sayyidah Hafsah (radhiyallahu 'anha), Sayyiduna 'Umar (radhiyallahu 'anhu) arrived. Noticing that someone was in the home with his daughter, he asked her, "Who is this?" She replied, "Asmaa bintu 'Umais (radhiyallahu 'anha)." Sayyiduna 'Umar (radhiyallahu 'anhu) asked, "Is she the one who lived in Abyssinia? The one who arrived via the ocean?" When she replied in the affirmative, Sayyiduna 'Umar (radhiyallahu 'anhu) remarked, "We preceded you in performing hijrah (to Madeenah Munawwarah), and hence we have a greater right to Rasulullah (sallallahu 'alaihi wasallam) than you."

Sayyidah Asmaa (radhiyallahu 'anha) was upset at this remark and retorted, "Never, by Allah! While you were with Rasulullah (sallallahu 'alaihi wasallam) who fed the hungry among you and taught the unlearned among you, we were in the distant land of the enemies. (Our migration to Abyssinia) was for the sake of Allah Ta'ala and Rasulullah (sallallahu 'alaihi wasallam)." She thereafter said, "I take an oath by Allah – I will neither eat a morsel nor drink a sip until I mention your remark to Rasulullah (sallallahu 'alaihi wasallam) and ask him (whether your remark is correct or not)." However, Sayyidah Asmaa (radhiyallahu 'anha) also mentioned, "By Allah! (When reporting your statement to Rasulullah [sallallahu 'alaihi wasallam],) I will neither lie, nor twist your words, nor add to your remark (i.e. I will report exactly what you said, word-for-word, nothing more and nothing less)."

Hence, she later went to Rasulullah (sallallahu 'alaihi wasallam) and reported what had transpired between her and Sayyiduna 'Umar (radhiyallahu 'anhu). Hearing this, Rasulullah (sallallahu 'alaihi wasallam) asked her, "What was your reply to him?" When she mentioned her response to Rasulullah (sallallahu 'alaihi wasallam), he said to her, "He does not have a greater right to me than you. He and his companions have performed one hijrah, whereas you, O people of the ship, have performed hijrah twice."

For the Sahaabah (radhiyallahu 'anhum) who had arrived from Abyssinia, this testament to their virtue, on the blessed tongue of Rasulullah (sallallahu 'alaihi wasallam) himself, held great importance and was an immense source of happiness.

(Saheeh Bukhaari #4230 & #4231 and Fat-hul Baari)

Lessons:

❀ Today, a person's greatest source of happiness may be his new car, or jewellery, or holiday trip, or house, etc. However, for the Sahaabah (radhiyallahu 'anhum), the greatest source of happiness was their progress in Deen and righteousness.

❀ As the lives of the Sahaabah (radhiyallahu 'anhum) revolved entirely around Deen, when they competed and vied with each other, it was also for progressing in Deen. For example, they never competed in acquiring wealth, but rather competed in spending their wealth for Deen.

❀ When Sayyidah Asmaa (radhiyallahu 'anha) went to report that remark of Sayyiduna 'Umar (radhiyallahu 'anhu) to Rasulullah (sallallahu 'alaihi wasallam), she ensured that she reported it verbatim, without exaggerating or misrepresenting the facts. The reason being that she was seeking the truth. On the contrary, a person will exaggerate and twist the facts when he is seeking to justify his own agenda.

Bidding her Husband Farewell

During the year 8 A.H., the momentous Battle of Mutah transpired. This was just a few months after Sayyidah Asmaa bintu 'Umais (radhiyallahu 'anha) and her husband, Sayyiduna

Ja'far (radhiyallahu 'anhu), arrived in Madeenah Munawwarah from Abyssinia.

When dispatching the army, Rasulullah (sallallahu 'alaihi wasallam) appointed Sayyiduna Zaid bin Haarithah (radhiyallahu 'anhu) as the commander of the army. However, Rasulullah (sallallahu 'alaihi wasallam) also mentioned, "If Zaid (radhiyallahu 'anhu) is killed, then Ja'far (radhiyallahu 'anhu) will be the commander, and if Ja'far (radhiyallahu 'anhu) is killed then 'Abdullah bin Rawaahah (radhiyallahu 'anhu) will be the commander. If 'Abdullah bin Rawaahah (radhiyallahu 'anhu) is killed, then the Muslims should appoint someone among themselves."

From this statement of Rasulullah (sallallahu 'alaihi wasallam), the Sahaabah (radhiyallahu 'anhum) understood that these three Sahaabah (radhiyallahu 'anhum) would be blessed with martyrdom in this battle. Subsequently, all of them were martyred by the enemy.

Sayyidah Asmaa (radhiyallahu 'anha) relates:

When Ja'far (radhiyallahu 'anhu) and his companions were martyred, Rasulullah (sallallahu 'alaihi wasallam) came to (break the news to) me. At the time when he came, I had tanned forty skins, had prepared the dough (for the daily bread) and had already bathed my children, applied oil on them and had seen to it that they were neat and tidy. When Rasulullah (sallallahu 'alaihi wasallam) arrived, he said to me, "Bring me the children of Ja'far (radhiyallahu 'anhu)." When I took the children to him, (out of love for them and pity for them,) he (sallallahu 'alaihi wasallam) began to inhale their smell, as his blessed eyes flowed with tears.

Seeing him weep, I asked, "O Rasul of Allah (sallallahu 'alaihi wasallam)! May my father and mother be sacrificed for you! Why are you weeping? Have you received some information regarding Ja'far (radhiyallahu 'anhu) and his companions?" Rasulullah (sallallahu 'alaihi wasallam) answered, "Yes, they were killed today." Rasulullah (sallallahu 'alaihi wasallam) then instructed his family, "Do not neglect to prepare food for the family of Ja'far (radhiyallahu 'anhu), as they will now be occupied with his death."

Three days later, Rasulullah (sallallahu 'alaihi wasallam) again went to visit the family of Sayyiduna Ja'far (radhiyallahu 'anhu). On this occasion, he (sallallahu 'alaihi wasallam) held the hand of his son, Sayyiduna 'Abdullah (radhiyallahu 'anhu), raised it and made the following du'aa thrice, "O Allah! Grant Ja'far (radhiyallahu 'anhu) a good replacement in his family, and grant 'Abdullah (radhiyallahu 'anhu) blessings in the transaction of his right hand (i.e. in all his transactions, as the right hand was generally used to conclude business deals)."

Sayyidah Asmaa (radhiyallahu 'anha) then mentioned her concern to Rasulullah (sallallahu 'alaihi wasallam), regarding her children being orphans (and the difficulty that she would face in supporting them). Rasulullah (sallallahu 'alaihi wasallam) consoled her saying, "How can you fear poverty for them, whereas I am their guardian in this world and the next?"

Thereafter, when the army was returning to Madeenah Munawwarah, Rasulullah (sallallahu 'alaihi wasallam) went out to receive them. As he entered Madeenah Munawwarah with the army, the children came running to meet them. Seeing them, Rasulullah (sallallahu 'alaihi wasallam) instructed, "Take the youngsters and let them ride with you on your animals, and give me the son of Ja'far (to carry with me)."

On the demise of Sayyiduna Ja'far (radhiyallahu 'anhu), Sayyidah Asmaa (radhiyallahu 'anha) recited the following poetry to mourn his passing:

I take an oath that my soul will remain grieved over you and my skin will continue to be covered in dust.

May those eyes be sacrificed for Allah Ta'ala that saw a youngster who could match him, as at the time of battle, he was most skilled in his attack, most fierce and most steadfast.

(Saheeh Bukhaari #4261, Majma'uz Zawaaid #10275 & #10282, Seerah Ibni Hishaam vol. 4, pg. 382 and Al-Bidaayah wan Nihaayah vol. 4, pgs. 270-283)

Lessons:

The Sahaabah (radhiyallahu 'anhum) were prepared to make any sacrifice for Deen and the pleasure of Allah Ta'ala. Hence, the men sacrificed their lives, the women sacrificed their husbands and the children sacrificed their fathers. **In the case of Sayyiduna Ja'far (radhiyallahu 'anhu), he had only been in**

Madeenah Munawwarah for a few months, and he and his family knew that he would probably not return, yet he still set out bravely, happy to give his life for Deen. At the very least, we should be prepared to sacrifice those things in our lives which displease Allah Ta'ala, be it music, movies, intermingling and chatting with non-mahrams, etc.

❀ When Sayyidah Asmaa (radhiyallahu 'anha) expressed her concern regarding her children's needs, Rasulullah (sallallahu 'alaihi wasallam) told her that she had no need to worry, as he was their guardian in this world and the next. When a person strives to always please Rasulullah (sallallahu 'alaihi wasallam) by adhering to his blessed sunnah and shunning sins, then he too will enjoy a special relationship with him. This special relationship will benefit him in this world and the next.

❀ On the death of Sayyiduna Ja'far (radhiyallahu 'anhu), Rasulullah (sallallahu 'alaihi wasallam) instructed his family to prepare food for them as they would be occupied with dealing with the tragedy. This is the teaching of Islam, that wherever possible, we try to bring comfort and assistance to people, especially in their hour of need. From this, we also understand that the 'funeral home' (home of the bereaved) should not become a 'function home', with other people eating meals there, as this causes great difficulty and inconvenience for the bereaving family who would have to attend to these people, see to their meals, etc.

The First Covered Bier in Islam

Sayyidah Faatimah (radhiyallahu 'anha), the blessed daughter of Rasulullah (sallallahu 'alaihi wasallam), and Sayyidah Asmaa bintu 'Umais (radhiyallahu 'anha) were sisters-in-law, as both of them were married to two brothers; Sayyiduna 'Ali bin Abi Taalib and Sayyiduna Ja'far bin Abi Taalib (radhiyallahu 'anhuma) respectively.

Shortly before she passed away, Sayyidah Faatimah (radhiyallahu 'anhu) mentioned to Sayyidah Asmaa bintu 'Umais (radhiyallahu 'anha), who was married to Sayyiduna Abu Bakr (radhiyallahu 'anhu) at that time, "O Asmaa! I do not like what is done with a woman's body (when she passes away and her body is being taken for burial, as merely) a cloth is placed on her body which allows her body shape to be seen."

Sayyidah Asmaa (radhiyallahu 'anha) replied, "O daughter of Rasulullah (sallallahu 'alaihi wasallam)! Shall I not show you something which I saw in the land of Abyssinia?" Saying so, she called for some fresh, moist palm leaves to be brought. When they were brought, she shaped them (into a funeral bier). Thereafter, she draped a cloth over the bier (and due to the frame, the cloth would not lie directly on the woman's body, thus concealing it's shape).

When Sayyidah Faatimah (radhiyallahu 'anhu) was shown the bier, she was so delighted that she exclaimed, "How excellent and beautiful this is! May Allah Ta'ala conceal you (i.e. your faults, O

Asmaa!) as you have concealed my body." In fact, such was her happiness that this was the only time that she was seen smiling (since the demise of her beloved father, Rasulullah [sallallahu 'alaihi wasallam], approximately six months prior to that).

After her demise, her body was carried on this bier, making her the first woman in Islam to be carried on this bier. The second was Sayyidah Zainab bintu Jahsh (radhiyallahu 'anha). In this way, Sayyidah Asmaa (radhiyallahu 'anha) provided a unique service to all the woman of this Ummah, assisting them to maintain their modesty after death as well.

(Mustadrak Haakim #4763, Usdul Ghaabah vol. 5, pgs. 368 & 369, Siyaru Aa'laamin Nubalaa vol. 2, pg. 132)

Lessons:

🌸 Even as she was approaching her final moments, one of the greatest concerns of Sayyidah Faatimah (radhiyallahu 'anha) was that of her modesty. Her concern was that even after death, her body should remain concealed from strange men, to the extent that not even the shape of her body be visible. When this was her concern to conceal her body even after death, the extent of her concern to conceal herself from strange men in her lifetime can be well imagined. This alone is sufficient in illustrating how crucial modesty is in the life of a Muslimah. Likewise, on seeing the bier, she experienced such happiness, knowing that her modesty would be protected, that it was the only time she was seen smiling since the demise of her beloved father (sallallahu 'alaihi wasallam).

❀ Sayyidah Asmaa (radhiyallahu 'anha), enjoyed such a close and loving relationship with her sister-in-law, **Sayyidah Faatimah** (radhiyallahu 'anha), that it was Sayyidah Asmaa (radhiyallahu 'anha) whom Sayyidah Faatimah (radhiyallahu 'anha) turned to at the end of her life, confiding in her and explaining her fear to her.

The Faithful Wife

Sayyidah Asmaa bintu 'Umais (radhiyallahu 'anha) was fortunate to have been married to the best of the Sahaabah (radhiyallahu 'anhum). Her first husband was Sayyiduna Ja'far (radhiyallahu 'anhu). After his martyrdom, she married Sayyiduna Abu Bakr (radhiyallahu 'anhu). Thereafter, her third husband was Sayyiduna 'Ali (radhiyallahu 'anhu). However, these three Sahaabah (radhiyallahu 'anhum) were also fortunate to be married to her, as she was not only pious, but was a most faithful and obedient wife, as is evident from the two incidents below:

- One day, while in the marriage of Sayyiduna 'Ali (radhiyallahu 'anhu), two of her children began to argue with one another regarding whose father was better. One was her son Muhammad (radhiyallahu 'anhu), from Sayyiduna Abu Bakr (radhiyallahu 'anhu), and the other was her son Muhammad (radhiyallahu 'anhu), from Sayyiduna Ja'far (radhiyallahu 'anhu). Each son said to the other, "I have more nobility than you, and my father was better than your father!"

On observing this, Sayyiduna 'Ali (radhiyallahu 'anhu) said to Sayyidah Asmaa (radhiyallahu 'anha), "O Asmaa, you pass the decision between them!" Sayyidah Asmaa (radhiyallahu 'anha) replied, "I never saw a youngster, from the Arabs, better than Ja'far (radhiyallahu 'anhu), and I never saw a middle-aged man better than Abu Bakr (radhiyallahu 'anhu)."

- When Sayyiduna Abu Bakr (radhiyallahu 'anhu) was about to pass away, he made a bequest that Sayyidah Asmaa (radhiyallahu 'anha) should carry out his ghusl upon his demise. However, he also gave her the instruction that she should break the (nafl) fast that she was keeping so that she would have the strength to carry out the ghusl. When Sayyiduna Abu Bakr (radhiyallahu 'anhu) passed away, she carried out the ghusl, but forgot to break her nafl fast and only remembered his instruction towards the end of the day. At that time, even though she had already carried out the ghusl, she broke her nafl fast, by drinking water, and remarked, "I will not follow the death of my husband today with disobedience to his instruction."

Note: It is permissible to break a nafl fast for a valid excuse. In this case, perhaps Sayyiduna Abu Bakr (radhiyallahu 'anhu) regarded this to be a valid excuse to break her nafl fast.

(Musannaf Ibni Abi Shaibah #32871 & #11079 and Tabaqaat Ibni Sa'd vol. 8, pgs. 284 & 285)

Lesson:

❀ Sayyidah Asmaa (radhiyallahu 'anha) had such faithfulness and loyalty to her husbands that she upheld their honour even after their demise. Hence, when asked to decide which of her first two husbands was the best, she ensured that she did not praise one at the expense of the other, but rather honoured each one of them without the other being dishonoured in any way.

Similarly, she ensured that she fulfilled the instruction of her husband, Sayyiduna Abu Bakr (radhiyallahu 'anhu), even after his demise. From these two incidents, it is clear that she possessed the qualities of faithfulness and obedience to the highest degree.

Steadfast in Adversity

Sayyiduna Muhammad bin Abi Bakr (radhiyallahu 'anhuma) was the son of Sayyidah Asmaa bintu 'Umais (radhiyallahu 'anha) from Sayyiduna Abu Bakr (radhiyallahu 'anhu).

During the era of his khilaafah, Sayyiduna 'Ali (radhiyallahu 'anhu) deputed Muhammad (radhiyallahu 'anhu) to Egypt as the governor of that region. However, sometime thereafter, he was mercilessly killed in Egypt. When the news of his death reached his mother, Sayyidah Asmaa (radhiyallahu 'anha), it caused her immense grief, but being the strong, resolute woman that she was, she immediately adopted sabr (patience) and resorted to her place of salaah within the home (where she poured her heart out to Allah Ta'ala).

Sayyidah Asmaa (radhiyallahu 'anha) once mentioned, "Rasulullah (sallallahu 'alaihi wasallam) taught me to recite the following words at the time of adversity:

اَللّٰهُ اَللّٰهُ رَبِّيْ لَا أُشْرِكُ بِهِ شَيْئاً

'Allah, Allah is my Rabb, I will not ascribe anything as partner to Him'."

(Sunan Abi Dawood #1525, Usdul Ghaabah vol. 4, pg. 76 and Al-Isaabah vol. 8, pg. 16)

Lesson:

🌷 No matter what happens to us in life, and how difficult the calamity may seem, the solution is to turn to Allah Ta'ala and pour our hearts out to Him in du'aa. Complaining to people will not achieve much, and in many cases, people will eventually become irritated and tired of our complaints.

Early Centuries of Islam

Piety in Public and in Privacy

During the period of his khilaafah, Sayyiduna 'Umar (radhiyallahu 'anhu) had passed a law prohibiting milk merchants from diluting their milk with water. The reason for this law was that many merchants would not inform people that the milk was diluted. Hence, the people would be deceived into thinking that the milk was pure and undiluted, and would thus pay the full price for it, whereas it was actually diluted.

One night, when Sayyiduna 'Umar (radhiyallahu 'anhu) was conducting his routine patrol through the streets of Madeenah Munawwarah, he felt a little tired. He thus paused his patrolling and rested for a few moments by leaning against a wall. While he was leaning against the wall, he overheard a mother instruct her daughter saying, "It is nearly morning already! Why are you not mixing the water into the milk?"

The daughter replied, "O my mother! Are you not aware of the law which Ameerul Mu-mineen passed today?" The mother asked, "What law did he pass?" The daughter answered, "He instructed someone to announce that mixing water into milk is not allowed."

Hearing this, her mother responded, "O my daughter! Go and mix the water into the milk, for you are in a place where neither 'Umar (radhiyallahu 'anhu) nor his announcer can see you! Furthermore, all the people are mixing water into their milk!"

Her daughter replied, "By Allah! I will not obey 'Umar (radhiyallahu 'anhu) in public and defy him in private! If 'Umar (radhiyallahu 'anhu) does not know, then the Rabb of 'Umar (radhiyallahu 'anhu) (certainly) knows!"

Unbeknownst to the mother and daughter, Sayyiduna 'Umar (radhiyallahu 'anhu) had overheard every word of their conversation. He turned to his freed slave, Aslam (rahimahullah), and said, "Mark this door and make a note of this location." Saying this, Sayyiduna 'Umar (radhiyallahu 'anhu) resumed his patrol.

The following morning, Sayyiduna 'Umar (radhiyallahu 'anhu) said to Aslam (rahimahullah), "Go to that place and find out the identity of the one speaking, as well as the one spoken to, and find out whether there is any male in their home." When Aslam (rahimahullah) made the relevant enquiries, he learnt that it was an unmarried daughter speaking to her mother, and there was no man in the home.

After receiving the report of Aslam's (rahimahullah) enquiries, Sayyiduna 'Umar (radhiyallahu 'anhu) summoned his sons and asked them, "Do any of you need to get married? There is a certain girl who is such that if I had the need to get married, I would have been the first to marry her." Two sons of Sayyiduna 'Umar (radhiyallahu 'anhu), 'Abdullah (radhiyallahu 'anhu) and 'Abdur

Rahmaan (radhiyallahu 'anhu), both replied that they were already married. However, his other son, 'Aasim (radhiyallahu 'anhu), replied, "O my father! I am unmarried, so marry me to her!"

Sayyiduna 'Umar (radhiyallahu 'anhu) also mentioned to 'Aasim (radhiyallahu 'anhu), "Select her to be your wife, for I have hope that through her, Allah Ta'ala will bless you (in your progeny) with a pious child like her that will become the leader of the Arabs."

The proposal was then sent and the nikaah was performed. From this union, a daughter named Ummu 'Aasim was born. She married 'Abdul 'Azeez bin Marwaan, who instructed his financial manager when marrying her, "Give me four hundred dinaars (gold coins) from the purest wealth that I possess, for I wish (to use it) to marry a woman who hails from a household of piety." It was from this marriage that 'Umar bin 'Abdil 'Azeez (rahimahullah) was subsequently born.

(Taareekh Ibni 'Asaakir vol. 70, pgs. 25 -254, Seerah 'Umar bin 'Abdil 'Azeez - Ibnu 'Abdil Hakam pg. 23)

Lessons:

Despite being the khaleefah of the Muslims, Sayyiduna 'Umar (radhiyallahu 'anhu) would personally patrol through the streets at night, faithfully serving his subjects. The reason for Sayyiduna 'Umar (radhiyallahu 'anhu) doing this was that he feared accountability and responsibility before Allah Ta'ala regarding the welfare of his subjects, and hence he wished to personally ensure that all was in order. In a similar manner, when we have children, then we will be accountable and responsible regarding their upbringing. In this regard, we need to show the same level of concern displayed by Sayyiduna 'Umar (radhiyallahu 'anhu).

❀ The quality the girl possessed, that impressed Sayyiduna 'Umar (radhiyallahu 'anhu), was her consciousness of Allah Ta'ala. Whether in private or public, behind closed doors or out in the open, she was fully conscious of Allah Ta'ala.

❀ When the mother reasoned saying, "All the people mix water into the milk," it did not deter, sway or influence the daughter. She understood that instead of looking at what people were doing, she needed to look at what Allah Ta'ala wanted her to do.

❀ When choosing a marriage partner, the quality of piety should never be overlooked. Rather, it should be the main motivating factor in the choice we make.

❀ Purity begets purity. Thus, 'Abdul 'Azeez bin Marwaan ensured that his nikaah was performed using pure wealth, as he wanted this nikaah to produce purity. The result speaks for itself, as 'Umar bin 'Abdil 'Azeez (rahimahullah) was born from this union of purity.

Righteousness is Always Rewarded

Salamah bin Kuhail (rahimahullah) was an eminent Taabi'ee and Muhaddith who had met the likes of Sayyiduna 'Abdullah bin 'Umar (radhiyallahu 'anhuma) and Sayyiduna Zaid bin Arqam (radhiyallahu 'anhu). The following incident is regarding his granddaughter, Bakh-khah.

Her brother recounts:

I had an elder sister who suffered a mental breakdown due to which she became withdrawn and reclusive. She stayed in a room at the far end of the attic, and remained there for more than ten years.

Despite her mental condition, she tried to always remain in the state of tahaarah (purity), and was particular about her salaah. On certain occasions, she would succumb to her condition and lose her sanity for a few days. However, on recovering her sanity, she would make a note of the number of salaahs which she had missed so that she could perform the qadhaa afterwards.

One night, while I was asleep, I heard a knock on my door around midnight. I called out, "Who's there?" to which I received the reply, "Bakh-khah." (To ensure that it really was her,) I asked, "My sister?" to which she responded, "Yes, your sister." I called out, "Welcome!" and stood, opening the door, allowing her to enter.

Seeing that she had not ventured (out of her room) into any portion of the house for more than ten years, I asked her, "O my sister, is everything fine?" She replied, "Yes, everything is fine."

She then related the following, "I had a dream tonight, in which someone greeted me with salaam. I replied to the salaam, after which the person said, 'Allah Ta'ala has looked after your father on account of your grandfather, and Allah Ta'ala will look after you on account of your father. Hence, if you wish, I will make du'aa to Allah Ta'ala on your behalf and He will remove your affliction. Alternatively, you can exercise patience if you wish, and you will be rewarded with Jannah. Sayyiduna Abu Bakr and Sayyiduna 'Umar (radhiyallahu 'anhuma) have both interceded to Allah Ta'ala on your behalf, due to the love which your father and grandfather had for them.'

I replied, 'If I am forced to choose between the two then I will choose to exercise patience over my condition in exchange of Jannah. However, Allah Ta'ala is most vast (in His generosity) and nothing is difficult for Him. If He wants to bless me with a complete recovery and also bless me with Jannah, He can easily do so.' The person replied, 'Allah Ta'ala has blessed you with both, and He is happy with your father and grandfather on account of their love for Sayyiduna Abu Bakr and Sayyiduna 'Umar (radhiyallahu 'anhuma). Stand and go!'" In this manner, Allah Ta'ala removed her affliction.

(Sifatus Safwah vol. 2, pg. 116)

Lessons:

- Pious parents and grandparents are an invaluable bounty. In many cases, although a person may not realize it, he is enjoying special barakah (blessings) and bounties of Allah Ta'ala on account of these individuals. It is only when they are deceased that he realizes the extent to which he benefited through them.

- Love for the Sahaabah (radhiyallahu 'anhum) is a requirement of imaan and is a very virtuous action. Every Muslim must engender love in his heart for the Sahaabah (radhiyallahu 'anhum) through reading inspirational incidents of their lives.

- Apart from the reward which a person will certainly receive in the Hereafter for his righteousness, he will often be rewarded in this world as well by being blessed with some special goodness, favour, etc. In some cases, one may not see this special favour in his lifetime, as Allah Ta'ala may bless his progeny with this special favour. Whatever the case, the point to remember is that no good deed goes unrewarded.

- We should never lose hope in the mercy of Allah Ta'ala. Even if we have a problem or affliction that has persisted for years and years, we should continue turning to Allah Ta'ala, as He can still change our condition.

❀ Allah Ta'ala is most generous, kind and loving. If we remain obedient and loyal to Him, He will open His treasures to us, and there is no limit to how much He can bless us with.

❀ Although Bakh-khah suffered from a mental condition for more than ten years, she never neglected her salaah, always performing her outstanding salaah when she regained her sanity. In the same way, we must make a resolution to always remain punctual on our salaah, and if we have any qadhaa (outstanding) salaahs, we must commence performing them immediately.

A Partner to Paradise

Riyaah bin 'Amr Qaisi (rahimahullah) was a student of the renowned saint, Maalik bin Dinaar (rahimahullah). He possessed such fear of Allah Ta'ala that he once said, "I have committed more than forty sins, for every one of these sins, I have recited istighfaar one hundred thousand times."

Riyaah was blessed to have married an exceedingly pious woman. On the first morning which he spent with his bride, she began kneading dough (to prepare bread). Observing this, he said, "Why do you not look for a woman to do this work for you?" She immediately (declined and) said, "The man I married is Riyaah Qaisi (rahimahullah) (i.e. a man known for piety). I do not think that I have married an obstinate tyrant (i.e. a man hankering after servants and the world)."

That night, Riyaah (rahimahullah) decided to test her. Hence, he went straight to bed after 'Esha Salaah, without performing any nafl salaah. His wife however, stood and commenced performing nafl salaah. After a quarter of the night had elapsed, she called out, "O Riyaah! Wake up (and engage in salaah)". He replied, "I am waking up," but remained in bed. After the second quarter of the night had elapsed, she again called out to him, "Wake up, Riyaah!" Once again, he replied, "I am waking up!" but did not leave the bed. When the third quarter had elapsed, she called out, "Wake up, O Riyaah!" When he again responded that he was waking up, but failed to leave the bed, she remarked, "The night is passing with the army of the righteous (engaged in righteousness), yet you remain asleep! If only I had not been deceived by the one who informed me about you (being a pious person)!" Saying this, she re-engaged in salaah, spending the last quarter of the night in 'ibaadah as well.

Her disinterest and disinclination towards the material was such, that once Riyaah (rahimahullah) became grieved over a worldly loss that he had suffered. Seeing him affected by this loss, his wife remarked, "I notice that you are grieving over something of the world. Shumait deceived me regarding you (being a pious and saintly person)." Saying this, she took hold of a tassel on her scarf and said, "The entire world is more worthless and insignificant in my sight than even this tassel!"

As for her dedication to her husband, Riyaah (rahimahullah) mentioned the following:

"After performing the 'Esha Salaah, she would apply perfume, wear (attractive) clothing and then present herself before me enquiring, "Do you have any need of me?" If I replied in the affirmative, then she would share the bed with me. Otherwise, she would remove the (attractive) clothing and stand in salaah until the morning. By Allah, she put me to shame!"

(Sifatus Safwah vol. 2, pgs. 218 & 255)

Lessons:

❁ One of the primary purposes of nikaah is to complete one's imaan and draw closer to Allah Ta'ala. Hence, when seeking a marital partner, one must ensure that they possess piety, as they will assist one along the path to Jannah. They will carry out righteous actions and encourage one to do the same, and if they see one committing any evil action, they will immediately prevent one from doing so. Such a marriage is not merely a 'marital relationship' – it is a partnership in the quest to earn Jannah.

❁ The wife of Riyaah (rahimahullah) understood that her obligation to her husband took precedence over nafl 'ibaadah. Hence, she would first adorn herself and present herself before her husband, and it was only if he had no need for her on that night would she spend the entire night in 'ibaadah. Similarly, despite spending the entire night in 'ibaadah, she happily attended to her domestic chores by herself. Understanding one's priorities in this manner is extremely essential. Otherwise, one may wrongly feel that one is gaining the proximity of Allah Ta'ala by doing something which is optional while neglecting an obligation.

❁ The material possessions of this world are a mere necessity of life and not the objective of one's existence. Hence, one should not become so consumed by worldly possessions, comforts and luxuries that one continuously chases after them and makes them the benchmark of one's success or failure.

Ummul Baneen (rahimahallah)

Piety in the Palace

When the lives of 'royal women' who led lives of piety are discussed, then in many instances, the first name to be mentioned is that of Faatimah bintu 'Abdil Malik (rahimahallah), the wife and cousin of 'Umar bin 'Abdil 'Azeez (rahimahullah). However, there was another 'royal woman' from the very same household who was also renowned for her piety. This woman was none other than Ummul Baneen (rahimahallah), the sister of 'Umar bin 'Abdil 'Azeez (rahimahullah) and cousin of Faatimah bintu 'Abdil Malik (rahimahallah).

Ummul Baneen (rahimahallah) was married to her cousin, Waleed bin 'Abdil Malik, who was the ruler of the Islamic empire during his time. Despite enjoying a position that made her the equivalent of a queen, she was not arrogant and filled with pride, nor was she intoxicated by the wealth and power that came with being married to the ruler. Instead, she always attributed the bounties and blessings that she enjoyed to Allah Ta'ala and acknowledged that it was on account of His favour alone that she enjoyed immense privilege and honour. It is for this reason that when she was once asked, "What is the most beautiful scene that you have ever beheld?" she replied, "The scene of Allah Ta'ala's favours being showered upon me."

Her devotion in salaah was also remarkable. She would often call some of her friends to come and spend time with her. They would then sit together and talk, enjoying each others' company. However, if her friends were engaged in conversation while she was performing salaah, she would be oblivious of their presence and would not hear even a single word of their conversation. She once mentioned to them, "I love speaking to you and thoroughly enjoy our conversations, but when I stand in salaah, I am completely oblivious of your presence and even forget that you are here."

Similarly, her time with her friends would not distract her from the remembrance of Allah Ta'ala or make her negligent of Him – let alone cause her to fall into the disobedience of Allah Ta'ala. Thus, she once mentioned, "When people are engaged in conversation, then there is nothing better with which they can adorn and beautify themselves with than the fear of Allah Ta'ala within their hearts."

Furthermore, despite hailing from the royal family and having servants at her beck and call, she did not consider it below her dignity to personally attend to the chores of the home. She was once seen preparing a pot of food. When she was asked about it, she replied, "It is a dish that Ameerul Mu-mineen (her brother, 'Umar bin 'Abdil 'Azeez [rahimahullah]) wished to eat, and so I am preparing it for him."

(Bahjatul Majaalis vol. 1, pg. 119, Sifatus Safwah vol. 2, pg. 431 and Taareekh Ibni 'Asaakir vol. 70, pg. 206)

Lessons:

🌸 No matter which family we come from or how much of wealth we may have, we must always remain humble and remember that everything is a favour of Allah Ta'ala. Furthermore, if He wishes, He can snatch away every blessing in the blink of an eye.

🌸 After imaan, it is the 'ibaadah of salaah that holds the greatest importance. Hence, we should invest our time and energy into perfecting our salaah, as this investment yields tremendous profits in this world as well as the next. However, this will only materialise if we give salaah its due importance. Instead of performing salaah as if we are 'merely doing it to get it over with', we should perform it with care, attention and the focus of the heart and mind.

🌸 When associating with friends, we should be ultra-cautious to ensure that we do not fall into sin, e.g. gossip and backbiting. In fact, we should try to make the meeting with our friends a means of us drawing nearer to Allah Ta'ala. One way to achieve this is for us to take some time out to speak about Allah

Ta'ala or read from some authentic Deeni books such as Fazaail-e-Aa'maal. Additionally, we must only keep the company of pious people, as it is hoped that their company will have an effect on our hearts and motivate us towards righteousness.

❁ To maintain love and ties with our family members, we do not have to buy expensive gifts for them. Sometimes, preparing a dish that they like and sending it for them is sufficient as a gesture of love to keep the hearts united.

❁ We should never consider it below our dignity to 'roll up our sleeves' and attend to the chores of the home.

Passion to Spend in the Path of Allah

Hailing from the ruling family and being married to the ruler of the time, Ummul Baneen (rahimahallah) had no shortage of wealth at her disposal. Despite this, her passion was to spend wealth in the path of Allah Ta'ala and not on herself. Hence, she was renowned for her charity and her spirit in assisting people in need.

In this regard, it seems as though Ummul Baneen (rahimahallah) followed in her father's footsteps and perhaps acquired this quality from him. The following statement of her father, 'Abdul 'Azeez bin Marwaan, highlights his spirit for charity. He says: "How surprising it is that a person has imaan, and is convinced that Allah Ta'ala provides for him and will replace that which he spends in His path, yet he still holds back his wealth from spending and thus deprives himself of abundant rewards!"

As for Ummul Baneen (rahimahallah), her own statement speaks volumes about the spirit of charity that burnt in her heart. She mentioned: "Every person has a passion in life, and my passion is to spend on people. By Allah! To maintain ties and relationships and to show compassion and sympathy to people is more beloved to me than delicious food at the time of hunger, and a cool drink at the time of thirst."

Some examples of her spending in the path of Allah Ta'ala are:

- She would free one slave every week.

- She would donate one horse every week to be used in the path of Allah Ta'ala. (Some narrations mention that she would free a slave and donate a horse every day, not every week!).

- When she invited her friends to spend time with her, before they would leave, she would gift them exquisite garments to wear. She would also give them gold coins and say, "The clothing is for you to keep, and the gold coins are for you to distribute amongst the poor among you."

Similarly, she condemned miserliness saying, "How despicable is miserliness! If miserliness was a path, I would not tread it, and even if it was the finest clothing, I would not wear it." She also mentioned, "The height of miserliness is where a person is too miserly to even purchase Jannah for himself."

(Al-Bidaayah wan Nihaayah vol. 9, pg. 207, Sifatus Safwah vol. 2, pg. 430 and Al-Mahaasin wal Masaawi vol. 1, pg. 144)

Lessons:

🌷 **One of the greatest challenges we face is that of protecting our hearts against the love of wealth.** When our hearts remain protected, we will spend the wealth in the correct avenues and thus become closer to Allah Ta'ala. However, if our hearts become saturated with the love of wealth, then this very same wealth will propel us towards sin through spending it in impermissible avenues and using it to show off, etc.

🌷 **It is an undeniable reality that children are a reflection of their parents, not only in their features but also in their habits.** When children grow up in a home where the parents are always giving sadaqah, engaged in the recitation of the Quraan Majeed, performing salaah, etc., then these same qualities rub off onto them. Hence, we need to be practical examples for our children.

🌷 **Spending in the path of Allah Ta'ala is an action that earns one ongoing rewards.** A person does not have to be a millionaire but can spend and contribute according to his own means – even if it is little. Allah Ta'ala looks at the heart with which the contribution is given. Hence, when there is an opportunity to spend in His path, we should hasten to spend whatever we can manage.

The Priority of Purity

On one occasion, Waleed bin 'Abdil Malik went to perform hajj with his wife, Ummul Baneen (rahimahallah). The governor of Yemen, Muhammad bin Yusuf, who was a tyrant oppressor like his brother Hajjaaj bin Yusuf, also came to perform hajj that very year.

He brought with him abundant gifts from Yemen for Waleed bin 'Abdil Malik. When Ummul Baneen (rahimahallah) learnt of this, she approached her husband (before Muhammad bin Yusuf could even present the gifts) and requested, "O Ameerul Mu-mineen! Please give me the gifts that Muhammad bin Yusuf has brought!" Her husband happily obliged and instructed that the gifts be given to her.

Accordingly, Ummul Baneen (rahimahallah) dispatched a few messengers to Muhammad bin Yusuf to inform him that the gifts should be sent to her instead of Waleed. Hearing this, Muhammad bin Yusuf was disappointed (as he probably wished to win favour with the ruler through his gifts) and refused saying, "Ameerul Mu-mineen must first see what I have brought. He may thereafter decide."

Thereafter, Ummul Baneen (rahimahallah) approached her husband and said, "O Ameerul Mu-mineen! Although you had given the instruction for the gifts of Muhammad bin Yusuf to be given to me, I do not want them." When Waleed asked her the reason, she explained, "I have heard that he acquired this wealth through usurping the belongings of people, putting them through difficulty and oppressing them."

When Muhammad bin Yusuf later brought the gifts to Waleed, he addressed him saying, "It has reached me that you have acquired these gifts through usurping the wealth of people!" Muhammad bin Yusuf immediately began to protest his innocence saying, "Allah forbid (that this allegation be true)!" Unsatisfied, Waleed commanded him to stand between the Hajr Aswad and the Maqaam Ebrahim and take fifty oaths, in the name of Allah Ta'ala, that he did not obtain any of the wealth by taking it from people unrightfully, nor did he oppress anyone, and that he had only acquired the wealth through pure and halaal sources.

After Muhammad bin Yusuf took the fifty oaths, Waleed made the gifts over to Ummul Baneen (rahimahallah) who then accepted them.

(Taareekh Tabari vol. 7, pg. 399)

Lesson:

As long as Ummul Baneen (rahimahallah) had a doubt regarding whether the gifts were taken from people unjustly, she refrained from accepting them. She only took the gifts when this doubt was cleared through Muhammad bin Yusuf taking the oaths. From this, it is apparent that she had great concern for her wealth to be halaal and pure. We too should similarly have the perpetual concern for halaal, whether in food or wealth. If we have the slightest doubt regarding whether something is halaal, we should leave it out.

Worried for the Welfare of Others

'Abdullah bin Qais was a renowned poet who had joined Mus'ab bin Zubair (rahimahullah) in fighting against 'Abdul Malik bin Marwaan. When Mus'ab bin Zubair (rahimahullah) was defeated, 'Abdullah bin Qais was forced to flee for his life, as the soldiers and police of 'Abdul Malik were relentlessly searching for him and were seeking to execute him. Eventually, 'Abdullah bin Qais fled from Kufah to Madeenah Munawwarah.

On his arrival in Madeenah Munawwarah, he went to the home of the Sahaabi, Sayyiduna 'Abdullah bin Ja'far (radhiyallahu 'anhuma), in the evening, covering his face so that no one would recognize him. When he entered the home, he found Sayyiduna 'Abdullah bin Ja'far (radhiyallahu 'anhuma) seated with some guests and about to partake of supper. He thus joined them in the meal. Once they had departed, 'Abdullah bin Qais exposed his face, allowing Sayyiduna 'Abdullah bin Ja'far (radhiyallahu 'anhuma) to recognise him.

On seeing him, Sayyiduna 'Abdullah bin Ja'far (radhiyallahu 'anhuma) exclaimed, "Is that you, Ibnu Qais?" When he replied in the affirmative, Sayyiduna 'Abdullah bin Ja'far (radhiyallahu 'anhuma) remarked, "How persistent and thorough they are in searching for you!" 'Abdullah bin Qais responded, "I have come to you seeking the protection of Allah Ta'ala and to ask you for your help and protection." Sayyiduna 'Abdullah bin Ja'far (radhiyallahu 'anhuma) replied, "They are desperate to apprehend you! I will try to protect you, and will write, on your behalf, to Ummul Baneen (rahimahallah), the daughter of 'Abdul 'Azeez, to intercede for you, as she is close to her uncle, 'Abdul Malik, who holds her in high regard."

Accordingly, Sayyiduna 'Abdullah bin Ja'far (radhiyallahu 'anhuma) sent a letter to Ummul Baneen (rahimahallah), asking her to intercede to her uncle, 'Abdul Malik, on behalf of 'Abdullah bin Qais. On receiving the letter, she went to 'Abdul Malik who asked if she needed anything. She replied, "Yes, I have one need." 'Abdul Malik was extremely intuitive and thus answered, "I have fulfilled every one of your needs, besides your request relating to 'Abdullah bin Qais." Ummul Baneen (rahimahallah) submitted, "Please, do not make this need an exception by not fulfilling it!"

At that moment, 'Abdul Malik raised his hand (perhaps in irritation), accidentally striking her on the cheek! She immediately clasped her cheek and remained silent, recovering from the blow. Seeing what had happened, 'Abdul Malik felt remorseful and relented saying, "I have accepted your request and he will now enjoy safety."

In this manner, Ummul Baneen (rahimahallah) managed to secure safety for 'Abdullah bin Qais, thus saving his life.

(Mir-aatuz Zamaan vol. 9, pg. 385 and Al-Faraj Ba'dash Shiddah vol. 2, pg. 350)

Lessons:

❀ Sayyiduna 'Abdullah bin Ja'far (radhiyallahu 'anhuma) and Ummul Baneen (rahimahallah) were both concerned about the safety and welfare of others. Hence, they tried their best to help the next person. In the case of Ummul Baneen (rahimahallah), interceding for 'Abdullah bin Qais could have caused her to lose her position and standing with her uncle as she knew that he hated 'Abdullah and wanted him killed. However, she took the risk and used her unique position and influence with 'Abdul Malik to try and help him. This is the spirit of Islam – every Muslim should try his utmost to help those in need in whichever way he can.

❀ Sometimes, a person may be in a unique position which gives them influence over certain people, as in the case of Ummul Baneen (rahimahallah). Instead of exploiting such a position to endlessly benefit ourselves, we should try to help people and promote works of righteousness and piety. By being instrumental in promoting Islam and Islamic values, our position and influence will be a blessing from Allah Ta'ala through which we will earn great reward.

Sorrow for her Statement

On one occasion, a woman named 'Azzah came to visit Ummul Baneen (rahimahallah). When 'Azzah entered, Ummul Baneen (rahimahallah) asked her "Kuthayyir recites the following poetry regarding you. What debt is he referring to in this poetry?"

> Every debtor whom I know has fulfilled his debt to his creditor. However, 'Azzah is procrastinating and distressing her creditor.

Initially, 'Azzah felt ashamed to discuss the matter and disclose what Kuthayyir was referring to, but when Ummul Baneen (rahimahallah) persisted, she said, "I had promised Kuthayyir that I would give him a kiss. However, (when I thereafter realized that it was a sin, I regretted making the promise and) I avoided fulfilling it."

When Ummul Baneen (rahimahallah) heard this, she remarked, "Fulfill the promise! I will bear the sin of your action."

After making this remark, Ummul Baneen (rahimahallah) realized that what she had said was absolutely impermissible. She thus sincerely repented to Allah Ta'ala and even freed forty slaves to compensate for this sin. Her sincerity and remorse was such that whenever she remembered this incident, she would weep and lament saying, "If only I had been dumb and had not uttered that statement!"

(Sifatus Safwah vol. 2, pg. 431)

Lessons:

❀   If a person decides to commit a sin, but thereafter has 'second thoughts', he should realize that this reluctance within him was inspired by Allah Ta'ala Who is helping him to resist the temptation. If he then plucks up the courage and resists committing the sin, Allah Ta'ala will reward him by recording a good deed for him. *(Saheeh Bukhaari #6491)* However, if one becomes indifferent and does not value this feeling of reluctance and continues to sin, a time may come when such inspiration will not come to him. Thereafter, he will plunge headlong into sin very easily without thinking twice.

❀   To avoid falling into sins through our tongues, we must train ourselves to think before we speak. Before we utter anything, we should first think whether the statement is sinful or not, and also ponder over the implications and repercussions of the statement. Finally, we should also think whether it is even necessary to utter the statement. If there is no need or benefit in saying it, then why do so? Ummul Baneen (rahimahallah) expressed the same remorse, of not pondering before speaking, when she lamented saying, "If only I had been dumb!"

❋ The sign of true repentance is that a person is overcome by remorse. If one makes taubah without remorse, his taubah will not be true taubah and he will not find any improvement or change in his life. The level of remorse that Ummul Baneen (rahimahallah) had can perhaps be gauged by the fact that she did not suffice on merely reciting "astaghfirullah" a few times, but also freed forty slaves as compensation. Hence, she was prepared to do whatever it took to make amends.

❋ Sin and the displeasure of Allah Ta'ala are extremely serious issues. We should never take them lightly and make remarks such as, "Never mind, I'll bear the sin!" In doing so, we are implying that we are not afraid of Allah Ta'ala's punishment and it does not worry us. Making light of a sin is far more serious than the sin itself.

Zubaidah (rahimahallah)

Leaving a Legacy

With every passing day, there are people who enter this world, taking their first breath and commencing the journey of life, and there are people who take their last breath and depart, never to return. However, from the billions of souls who came and went, only a select few left such a legacy that they earned themselves an entry in the pages of history.

One such person was a woman who was named Amatul 'Azeez, but was more commonly known as Zubaidah. It is reported that her grandfather, the famous Abbasid ruler, Abu Ja'far Mansoor, had given her the nickname Zubaidah on account of her radiant and beautiful complexion.

She was the wife of the renowned Khaleefah, Haaroon Rasheed whom she had married in 165 A.H. Apart from her husband being a powerful ruler and khaleefah, her son, known as Al-Ameen, and many of her close family members were also rulers of the Muslims. She thus enjoyed a position of distinction in the ruling family.

(Wafayaatul Aa'yaan vol. 2, pg. 314, Al-Muntazam vol. 8, pg. 278 and Taareekhul Islam vol. 15, pg. 156)

Hereunder, we will discuss her qualities, outstanding generosity and the long-standing legacy which she left for the Ummah.

The Passion to Share

On one occasion, the finance manager of Zubaidah (rahimahallah) learnt that an employee who administered her various properties, had taken funds from the revenue of her properties equivalent to two hundred thousand dirhams (silver coins). He thus had the man imprisoned for the crime.

While in prison, the man contacted two of his friends requesting them to approach the finance manager and intercede on his behalf. On the way, they met Faidh bin Abi Saalih who asked them, "Where are you going to?" They narrated the incident that had transpired and explained the purpose of their errand. "Do you need me to assist you?" he offered. The two friends expressed that they would appreciate his assistance, and so he accompanied them.

They gained an audience with the finance manager and pleaded their friend's case. He then sent a message to Zubaidah (rahimahallah), informing her about the situation. After reading the message, she initially replied, "There is no way that he can be released without paying the money that he owes." On hearing her response, the two friends rose to leave. However, Faidh remarked, "It would seem that our coming here has only served to further confirm the detention of your friend!" He then took an ink pot and wrote a message to his own financial manager, instructing him to pay the outstanding amount on the prisoner's behalf.

When Zubaidah's (rahimahallah) finance manager wrote her a message, apprising her of the turn of events, she returned the note to him with the following written on the reverse, "It is more befitting for us to show the prisoner this generosity. Return the money to Faidh and release the prisoner."

(Al-Muntazam vol. 10, pg. 277)

Lessons:

❀ Sometimes, an opportunity to do good comes our way, yet for some reason or other (be it anger, disappointment, etc.), we deflect or turn it away. However, so long as the opportunity has not passed, we can still relent and seize it. After our initial emotions subside, we can still capitalize and earn ourselves reward, as Zubaidah (rahimahallah) did when she relented.

❀ Instead of competing in holiday destinations, fashion, jewellery, etc., Zubaidah (rahimahallah) was competing in generosity. Since the prisoner was her debtor, she wanted to be the one to show the generosity instead of Faidh.

❀ Every person should try, within his means, to use his money for the benefit of others. It should never be that we have hearts of stone, where we are unprepared to share even a few rands with the next person. If we are enjoying wealth, we must remember that it is only due to Allah Ta'ala favouring us, and had He wished, He could have deprived us and favoured someone else instead. Hence, out of gratitude to Allah Ta'ala, let us have the heart to share with others – especially if it is to support righteous works and efforts, as this will earn us a share in these endeavours as well.

❀ When Faidh saw the two friends proceeding to the finance manager to intercede on behalf of their friend, he offered to help them, even though it was not his problem or concern. This shows the true spirit of a believer – he is always eager to bring comfort and ease to others.

❀ When their intercession initially failed, Faidh was prepared to pay the money himself – which was the considerable sum of two hundred thousand dirhams (silver coins) – to secure the release of the prisoner. This speaks volumes of the heart of compassion that he must have had.

Determined to Make a Difference

During the era of Zubaidah (rahimahallah), there was a scarcity of water in Makkah Mukarramah. This shortage was especially devastating at the time of hajj as during this period, thousands of people would flock to the blessed city, as well as the plains of 'Arafaat, Muzdalifah and Mina, from all corners of the Muslim world. Eventually, the demand for water was so high that people would pay up to one dinaar (gold coin) for a single bag of water!

When Zubaidah (rahimahallah) witnessed this, she was overcome with pity for the plight of the poor who could not afford this exorbitant amount, yet required this valuable resource for survival. She thus embarked on a project to provide water to the people in Makkah Mukarramah.

She summoned engineers and instructed them to survey the land around Makkah Mukarramah to locate viable sources from which water could be brought into Makkah Mukarramah. After conducting a detailed survey, the engineers proposed that water be brought via aqueducts (water channels) from Waadi Hunain and Waadi Nu'maan, as these two areas experienced more frequent rainfall, causing the groundwater level in those regions to be higher.

When Zubaidah's (rahimahallah) financial manager learnt of her intention, he cautioned her saying, "This project will be extremely costly!" She replied, "Go ahead with the project, even if it costs one dinaar (gold coin) for every strike of the axe (during its construction)!"

The engineers first brought water from Waadi Hunain. They dug wells in the area (to access the water) and brought the water to Makkah Mukarramah via an aqueduct. Huge tanks were constructed to store the water, the remains of which still exist today. However, after some time, the water at Waadi Hunain became depleted. Nevertheless, by this time, the supply of water could be met from Waadi Nu'maan.

Waadi Nu'maan is situated at the base of Jabal (Mount) Kara, 10km south-east of 'Arafaat, in the direction of Taa-if. Four or five wells were dug here, some up to 34m in depth! The water from all these wells would collect in a central well via small tunnels that were dug inbetween and an aqueduct was built to transport the water to Makkah Mukarramah.

As there were no pumps at the time, the water had to flow naturally, using the force of gravity. To make this possible, the aqueduct had to maintain a slight but constant slope all the way to Makkah Mukarramah! Hence, at times, the aqueduct was above the ground (e.g. along the hills of Muzdalifah), and at times, it tunnelled beneath the ground and even through the mountains. Small access wells were built at 50m intervals for the purpose of maintaining and cleaning the well (men who were small in built would enter the aqueduct at these points and attend to the cleaning, removal of blockages, etc.). The entire aqueduct, above and below ground, was solidified with a mortar made from lime and stones which made it waterproof.

From Waadi Nu'maan, the aqueduct first came to 'Arafaat. At Jabalur Rahmah, it stood approximately 3m high. Here, three tanks were constructed, as well as a drinking fountain (the remains of which can still be seen today). From 'Arafaat, the aqueduct proceeded to Muzdalifah where it took the shape of a well near Masjid Mash'arul Haraam. It was from this well that water would be taken to Mina for the hujjaaj. The aqueduct constructed by Zubaidah (rahimahallah) did not flow all the way into Makkah Mukarramah, but ended in the area known today as 'Azeeziyyah. In this area, the aqueduct ended in a large pond known as the Pond of Zubaidah (rahimahallah). Today, Masjid Shaikh Bin Baaz stands in this place. Commencing in Waadi Nu'maan and ending in 'Azeeziyyah, the aqueduct was approximately 38km in length!

The effectiveness of the aqueduct can be gauged from the fact that on a daily basis it would bring to Makkah Mukarramah, water equivalent to 160 tankers! The canal of Zubaidah (rahimahallah) continued to function until 1950 when due to the excessive amount of water that was being drawn out by pumps, the water became depleted at the source and the canal seized to flow. Hence, the canal continued to service the people of Makkah Mukarramah for approximately 1200 years!

One day, while the canal was under construction, Zubaidah's (rahimahallah) financial manager mentioned, "Four hundred thousand dirhams (silver coins) have already been spent on this project!" She responded, "You are only saying this because you wish to make me feel remorseful and discourage me from spending further in avenues of goodness! Continue to spend on it and complete the project, even if the cost is many times this amount!"

When the project was finally completed, ten years after its inception, the scribes came before her to officially record the cost of the project, which was in the region of 1.7 million dinaars (based on the current gold value, this equals approximately R8 billion!). However, she stopped them and said, "Leave the record for the Day of Record (i.e. I am not concerned over the cost, but I wish to see whether any reward has been recorded in my favour for undertaking this project)." She then instructed them to erase all records of the expenditure undertaken for this project.

(Wafayaatul Aa'yaan vol. 2, pg. 314, Al 'Iqduth Thameen vol. 6, pg. 398 and http://tiny.cc/zubaidah)

Lessons:

❀ When Zubaidah (rahimahallah) saw the people in difficulty, she could not sit by idly and ignore their plight. Instead, she used her unique resources, position and influence to bring relief to the people. Today, the world refers to a person with this spirit as a 'humanitarian'. However, we refer to such a person as a 'Muslim', as every Muslim should have this heart.

❁ Despite her financial manager's attempts to dissuade her on numerous occasions, she remained resolute and undeterred. This is the type of resolve and determination we should adopt when intending to carry out a good deed or when refraining from a sin.

❁ Perhaps one reason for Zubaidah's (rahimahallah) instruction to erase the official records is that she did not want to view the amount spent by her and be overcome by pride.

At the Forefront of Relief Efforts

As mentioned previously, Zubaidah (rahimahallah) had spearheaded and financed the unprecedented project of digging a water canal in Makkah Mukarramah. Although this was perhaps her most well-known charitable contribution, there were numerous other projects which she undertook in an effort to spend her wealth in avenues of virtue and righteousness.

One such example is that of a traveller's inn which she constructed in the mountainous region of Baghraas (south eastern Turkey). Any traveller coming to the city of Baghraas was welcome to reside at this inn, and she had dedicated the income of many waqf properties to the upkeep and maintenance of this inn.

The second project, for which she is also very well-known, is that of Darb Zubaidah (the Road of Zubaidah). Darb Zubaidah was a 1200km road that ran from Baghdad to Makkah Mukarramah, passing through Kufah and many other places such as Najaf, Qaadisiyyah, etc.

As Baghdad was the capital of the khilaafah and the center of the Islamic Empire at the time, numerous people from this region would travel to Makkah Mukarramah to perform hajj. Many of them were poor and travelled on foot, or were ill equipped and thus experienced difficulties in navigating this long road to Makkah Mukarramah. In fact, many of those traveling for hajj would die of thirst on the way or lose their lives due to becoming lost in the desert (as the road did not have markers initially).

Although Zubaidah (rahimahallah) did not build this road, she was responsible for the many improvements and facilities that were added to it. They include wells and water pools that were dug at regular distances, shelters built for travellers to rest under, deploying soldiers to accompany caravans, lighting fire beacons at night to guide travellers, marking the qiblah for travellers to perform salaah, and having a map of the entire 1200km road drawn by her engineers. In fact, it is probably due to her contributions to this road being the greatest that it became known by the title Darb Zubaidah.

Though more than 1200 years have passed, many of the wells and other structures that she built still exist – a testimony to the fact that no penny was spared in building them, as they were meant to last and to continue benefiting people.

Ibnu Batootah (d. 779 A.H.), the renowned explorer, journeyed on this road and mentioned, "Every structure, pond or well that is found on this road between Baghdad and Makkah Mukarramah is a result of the generosity of Zubaidah (rahimahallah) – may Allah Ta'ala reward her in full. If it were not for her concern and contribution to this road, nobody would have travelled on it."

Another famous traveller and geographer, Ibnu Jubair (d. 614 A.H.), echoed similar sentiments saying, "These structures, pools, wells and inns that are found on the road from Baghdad to Makkah Mukarramah are the product of Zubaidah (rahimahallah), the daughter of Ja'far, and wife and cousin of Haaroon Rasheed. She remained dedicated to (the improvement, upkeep and maintenance of) these facilities throughout her life. Hence, she left on this road various facilities and amenities that are for the benefit of all those traveling for hajj every year, from the time of her demise until now. If it was not for her generous contributions on this road, no person would travel on it."

(Hudoodul 'Aalam pg. 129, Rihlah Ibni Batootah pg. 189, Rihlah Ibni Jubair pg. 162, http://tiny.cc/zubaidah, http://tiny.cc/zubaidah_1 and http://tiny.cc/zubaidah_2)

Lessons:

❀ One of the remarkable qualities that stand out in the life of Zubaidah (rahimahallah) is the fact that although she was royalty, living in a palace with hundreds of servants at her beck and call, she never forgot the people who were poor and underprivileged. Rather, she went out of her way to help them. Furthermore, she was not content to help them in a small or meagre way, rather she desired to help them to the best of her ability. Hence, she spared no effort and embarked on massive projects which cost a fortune, but continued to benefit people at large for hundreds of years, reaping her tremendous rewards even after her demise.

❀ Sometimes, a person is blessed to complete a huge project for people's welfare but thereafter becomes complacent, as he feels that he has already earned his Jannah. When we look at Zubaidah (rahimahallah), however, we see that she never stopped striving for the Hereafter. After one huge project, she embarked on another, until she passed away. This is the demand of imaan – that we strive until the grave.

❀ There are many people whom Allah Ta'ala has blessed with abundant wealth. Often, such people think to themselves, "We've got the money, so if we don't spend it, what else will we do with it? We may as well enjoy it!" With this reasoning, they embark on holiday after holiday, "shop till they drop" and splurge money on countless other indulgences (visits to spas, restaurants, etc.). However, we choose to forget that there are many other things that we can do with our money – such as follow the example of Zubaidah (rahimahallah) and alleviate the sufferings of others.

Respecting the Symbols of Islam

Zubaidah (rahimahallah), although remembered by most for her generosity and charitable works, possessed another very important quality – that of honouring and showing importance to the salient symbols of Islam. She had a particular love for the Quraan Majeed and the azaan and would honour them both greatly.

She had appointed one hundred female attendants, who had memorized the Quraan Majeed, to recite three juz (paras) of the Quraan Majeed in her palace every day. Due to the number of people reciting, her palace would resonate with the sound of the Quraan Majeed, like a bee hive filled with buzzing bees.

Zubaidah (rahimahallah) passed away in the year 216 A.H. in Baghdad. After her demise, someone saw her in a dream and asked her, "How did Allah Ta'ala deal with you?" She replied, "Allah Ta'ala forgave me." She was asked, "Were you forgiven on account of the wells that you dug, the structures and facilities that you built and the other services that you rendered on the road to Makkah?" When she replied, "No," she was then asked, "On account of which action were you then forgiven?" She answered, "One day, I was seated and my handmaidens were singing before me when we suddenly heard the voice of the muazzin calling out the azaan. I immediately stopped them from singing and said to them, 'Reply to the azaan.' After I passed away, Allah Ta'ala made me stand before Him and then announced to the angels, 'O my angels! This is Zubaidah (rahimahallah), the one who remembered Me in the midst of her enjoyment. I make you witness that I have forgiven her.'"

(Wafayaatul Aa'yaan vol. 2, pg. 314 & 317 and Mir-aatuz Zamaan vol. 14, pg. 157)

Lessons:

We can never be complacent or confident regarding our outcome in the Hereafter, as we do not know if our actions will gain the acceptance of Allah Ta'ala. Hence, we should continue to strive, and never consider any good deed to be trivial or insignificant. It could be that an action which we regard to be small is actually very beloved to Allah Ta'ala and thus becomes the means of our salvation. In the case of Zubaidah (rahimahallah), even though she would have been rewarded greatly for her charitable works, it was the apparently 'small' act of her respect for the azaan that was greatly appreciated by Allah Ta'ala.

❀ To show honour, respect and importance to the salient symbols of Islam is, in actual fact, showing honour and respect to Allah Ta'ala. Hence, we should show the utmost importance to the masaajid, the Ka'bah, the Quraan Majeed, the azaan and anything else which is a symbol of Islam.

❀ When hearing the azaan, we should immediately adopt complete honour and respect for it. We should cease all conversation, ensure that our heads are covered and respond to the azaan.

❀ Every Muslim must honour and respect the Quraan Majeed. However, honouring the Quraan Majeed does not only entail handling it with respect and care. It also requires that we recite it regularly. Hence, every person should take out time daily to recite a portion of the Quraan Majeed.

❀ Many people remember Allah Ta'ala and turn to Him in times of difficulty. However, the sign of true love and loyalty is that the servant turns to Him and remembers Him in times of enjoyment and happiness as well.

Cautious in Consumption

Abul Hasan Makki (rahimahullah) had a daughter, living in Makkah Mukarramah, who was even more pious than him. Such was her simplicity and austerity that she lived and survived on a mere thirty dirhams (silver coins) for the year. Her father would send her this sum from the profit he made by selling mats woven by him from palm leaves.

The neighbour of Abul Hasan Makki (rahimahullah), Ibnur Rawwaas, relates the following:

I intended leaving for hajj, and so I went to Abul Hasan (rahimahullah) to bid him farewell, to ask if he needed anything, and to also request his du'aas. He handed me a paper bag and requested, "Ask the people of Makkah Mukarramah to direct you to so-and-so woman in such-and-such a location and hand this to her." I understood that the parcel was for his daughter.

I accepted the paper bag and on arriving in Makkah Mukarramah, I made enquiries regarding the woman. I discovered that her 'ibaadah and disinterest in the world had become so famous among the people that she was known by one and all. I thus decided to add some of my own money to the money that her father had sent so that I would also have a share in the reward. However, since I anticipated that she would not accept money from me, I opened the paper bag and secretly increased the amount from thirty coins to fifty, thereafter resealing the bag.

When I handed her the bag, she asked me, "How is my father?" I replied, "He is well." She thereafter remarked, "It seems as though he has begun to spend time in the company of the people of the world, and he has abandoned dedicating himself to Allah Ta'ala." She then said, "I wish to ask you something, so I beseech you, in the name of Allah Ta'ala, that Being for Whom you are performing hajj, to answer me truthfully." I responded, "Certainly!"

She asked, "Did you mix some of your own wealth into this money?" I answered, "Yes, but how did you know?" She said, "My father would not give me more than thirty dirhams, as he cannot afford to give me more than that. The only way that he could have given me more would have been if he had given up his dedication to 'ibaadah (and spent more time in earning wealth). If you had informed me that this was indeed the case with my father then I would not have taken anything from his wealth either."

Having said this, she addressed me saying, "Take the entire amount of money away, for you have not fulfilled your duty towards me (of discharging the trust of the money to me), despite being able to do so." In response, I asked her, "How is this?" She replied, "I will not consume any wealth unless it was earned by myself or by my father. Likewise, I will not accept any wealth unless I am able to verify its condition (i.e. whether it was earned through halaal sources or otherwise)."

I responded saying, "In that case, take the thirty dirhams which your father sent for you and return the rest." She retorted, "If I was able to identify those exact coins, from all the other coins, then I would certainly do so. However, my father's coins have now been mixed with the other coins (and I cannot separate them). Hence, I will not accept any of the coins. Now, I will have to live off the dumps in order to survive until the next hajj season (when my father will send money again), as this money was my allowance for the entire year. You have put me into hunger (and difficulty). Had your intention not been to assist me, I would have cursed you."

After completing my hajj, I returned to Basrah, grieved and remorseful over what had transpired. I went to Abul Hasan (rahimahullah), informed him of what had happened and apologized to him. (After hearing me out,) he said, "I will not take this money from you either, as it has now been mixed with the other coins (and cannot be separated). You have been undutiful to me and to her." (Completely at a loss,) I asked him, "What should I do with the coins?" "I don't know," he replied.

I persevered for some time, continuously apologizing to him and asking him what I should do with the money, until he eventually said, "Give it in sadaqah." I thus gave it in charity.

(Sifatus Safwah vol. 1, pg. 448)

Lessons:

- What a person consumes has a direct impact and effect on his actions, the condition of his heart and his motivation towards righteousness. Furthermore, 'what we consume' is not restricted to the food we eat, but includes the wealth that we earn, etc. It is for this reason that the pious people of the past would exercise such caution regarding their wealth.

- The pious do not only abstain from that which is clearly impermissible, but also refrain from that which is doubtful. Likewise, if they are unable to verify that something is completely halaal (e.g. due to lack of information, the inability to inquire, etc.) then they exercise caution and refrain from it.

- The purpose of doing someone a favour is to bring comfort to that person. Hence, before doing the favour, we must ensure that the person will be comfortable with what we are doing. Otherwise, we may assume that we are doing him a favour, whereas we may be actually doing him a disservice and causing him inconvenience. If we know a person very well, then we will be acquainted with their temperament and will be able to bring them comfort. However, if we are not well acquainted with their temperament, we should rather enquire before doing anything, as we may unintentionally put the person through difficulty despite meaning well.

The Gleaming Jewel

There was once a slave girl named Jowharah (rahimahallah) (which means 'jewel'). She initially belonged to a certain king, but was thereafter freed. After gaining her emancipation, she renounced the world and married Abu 'Abdillah Al-Baraathi (rahimahullah). She then dedicated her life to remaining engaged in the 'ibaadah of Allah Ta'ala. The following are two incidents which shine in the life of this gleaming jewel:

On one occasion, Jowharah (rahimahallah) asked her husband, "O Abu 'Abdillah! Will women be adorned with jewellery when they enter Jannah?" When he replied in the affirmative, she suddenly emitted a shriek and collapsed unconscious. When she regained her senses, her husband asked her, "What happened?" She replied, "I remembered my previous condition and lifestyle, and all the luxuries of the world that I had acquired. By Allah, I feared that I would be deprived of abundant rewards in the Hereafter!"

One night, Jowharah (rahimahallah) had a dream in which she saw magnificent tents erected. She enquired, "Who are these tents for?" She was informed, "It is for those who recite the Quraan Majeed in Tahajjud Salaah." After seeing this dream,

Jowharah (rahimahallah) dedicated her entire night to performing Tahajjud Salaah.

She would also awaken her husband at night to perform Tahajjud Salaah and would say, *"Kaarwaan raft."* **(a statement in Persian meaning 'the caravan has departed'. What she meant was that they should not be left behind, but should also join the caravan of the people of Jannah, by performing Tahajjud Salaah).**

(Sifatus Safwah vol. 1, pg. 575)

Lessons:

🌷 The purpose of a person's life is to prepare and develop his Jannah. While we are allowed to enjoy the permissible pleasures and luxuries of this world, we should not allow these to distract us and become an impediment in our path to paradise by causing us to neglect fulfilling the rights of Allah Ta'ala and the people, and by causing us to fall into sin.

🌷 In life, people generally fear 'being left behind'. However, this fear is with regards to the latest fashions and fads, holiday destinations, cars, etc. that they fear being left behind from. In reality, even if we do not get 'left behind' with regard to these things, we will have to 'leave them behind' when we pass away one day. Hence, we should rather worry about not being left behind on the journey to Jannah.

Every person is able to influence and encourage others towards good in some way or another, but a wife has a unique position in influencing her husband. Due to his attachment and fondness for her, he will often accept encouragement from her which he would not accept from other people. She should thus take full advantage of this privilege to assist him in reaching Jannah.

Grateful before the Giver

Abu Bilaal Aswad recounts the following:

I once set out on the journey of hajj. After traveling some distance, I encountered a woman who had neither a conveyance to ride nor a utensil to use. I asked her, "Where are you from?" She replied, "I am from the land of Balkh."

I then remarked to her, "I see that you neither have any provisions, nor a utensil in which you can carry provisions." She responded, "When I departed from Balkh, I had ten dirhams (silver coins) with me. I still have some of that amount." Hearing this, I asked her, "What will you do when the money is depleted?" She replied, "This cloak that I am wearing is extra. I will sell it, and then use the money to buy a cheaper cloak. I will then use the surplus money to see to my needs."

I next asked her, "What will you do when that amount is depleted?" She answered, "I will sell my scarf and purchase a cheaper one, using the surplus money to see to my needs." To this, I asked, "And what will you do when that amount is depleted?" She retorted, "O useless one! I will ask Allah Ta'ala and He will see to my needs!" I replied, "Why do you not make du'aa to Him before that (i.e. before your money is depleted and you are forced to sell your cloak and scarf)?" She responded, "Woe to you! I am ashamed to ask Allah Ta'ala for anything material while I already possess more material possessions than I require!"

I thereafter said to her, "Have a turn to ride upon my donkey for some time." In reply, she said, "Leave it." I thus left the donkey with her and remained behind for some errand that I had. After completing my errand, I resumed the journey, hastening behind the woman, following her tracks. However, I found only my donkey, standing with its saddlebags full. In these saddlebags, I found white flour that was better than any flour I had ever seen before. I sought the woman and searched for her, but I was unable to find her."

(Sifatus Safwah vol. 2, pg. 343)

Lessons:

🌸   When a person has true imaan, his conviction in Allah Ta'ala being the Sole Provider becomes so strong that he does not become overly concerned for wealth and material possessions. Rather, he turns to Allah Ta'ala and firmly believes that Allah Ta'ala will see to his needs, just as He sees to the needs of the birds and all other creatures.

🌸   The woman had such a strong sense of shukr (gratitude) for the few items that she possessed, that she considered it an act of ingratitude to still ask Allah Ta'ala for more while she enjoyed these bounties. On the other hand, we possess so many material bounties, yet remain ungrateful and still hanker after more.

Uninfluenced by Others

There was once a man who intended travelling to a certain place for work. However, his neighbours, for some reason, did not want him to leave home.

To achieve their goal and keep him home, they approached his wife in an attempt to influence her saying, "How can you allow him to leave you and travel? He has not even left any finances for you!" The wife calmly replied, "Ever since I have known my husband, I have known him to be the means through which the food comes home – not the one who actually provides the food. The One Who provides for me is my Rabb, Allah Ta'ala. If my husband, who is only the means of the food coming home, is not here, then Allah Ta'ala Who provides the food is still here to provide for me (and He can send it home through some other means).

(Ihyaau 'Uloomid Deen vol. 2, pg. 80)

Lessons:

❀ Allah Ta'ala alone is the Provider. When we have firm conviction in this, we will not be tempted to stretch our hands towards impermissible wealth, and we will realize that the key to solving our problems is to please Allah Ta'ala and turn to Him in du'aa.

❀ Often, a couple enjoy a happy and fulfilling marriage. However, others interfere in the marriage and 'create' unhappiness. **They sow grieviences in the wife's mind which was not there previously and thus poison her mind, until she is convinced that her marriage is one of unhappiness – even though she was happy just days before!** For our own sakes and that of our marriages, we need to guard ourselves against these influences by not listening or entertaining such ideas. **We should instead focus on the happiness that we enjoy and express gratitude to Allah Ta'ala and to our husbands for this. We should also avoid indulging in such behaviour – even if unintentionally.**

❀ Even though a husband may have certain faults, a loyal wife will not discuss them with all and sundry and reveal his shortcomings to others. **Instead, she will try to safeguard his dignity and honour, just as she would expect him to do the same for her.**

Latter Centuries of Islam

Wife of Moulana Qaasim Naanotwi (rahimahullah)

The Silent and Unseen Pillar

Moulana Muhammad Qaasim Naanotwi (rahimahullah) was an illustrious 'Aalim of the 19th century, and is a descendant of Sayyiduna Abu Bakr Siddeeq (radhiyallahu 'anhu). Moulana Qaasim (rahimahullah) only lived for 47 years, passing away in the year 1879, but left a legacy that continues to this day.

Moulana (rahimahullah) was blessed by Allah Ta'ala to render various services for Deen and the Muslims. However, from all his Deeni services, it is perhaps his founding of Darul 'Uloom Deoband that stands out the most. This institute, located in Deoband, India, has tens of thousands of graduates around the world, and many Deeni institutes today, in South Africa and abroad, are offshoots of this prestigious Darul 'Uloom and remain affiliated to it.

Moulana (rahimahullah) was blessed with proverbial piety, outstanding asceticism and true devotion to 'ibaadah. Similarly, his wife was an exceptionally pious woman who was blessed with many sterling qualities. Being the wife of Moulana (rahimahullah), she would have naturally made many sacrifices and supported him in every way possible to assist him in his endeavour to start the madrasah. She was the 'silent' and 'unseen' support and pillar in the foundation of this illustrious Darul 'Uloom, thus securing a share in the reward of all the good that continues to stem from it. Allah Ta'ala also honoured her by accepting her progeny to serve Deen in various ways.

Hereunder are some of the outstanding qualities of this remarkable woman so that we may inculcate these qualities in ourselves, thereby bringing true quality to our lives.

Taking out Time

The respected wife of Moulana Qaasim (rahimahullah) bore him ten children – three sons and seven daughters. We can therefore imagine the extent to which she remained occupied in looking after the children and raising them, together with her many other domestic responsibilities. Nevertheless, this saintly woman was such that despite all her responsibilities, she was always motivated towards piety and eager to engage in works of righteousness.

No matter what she may have been engaged in, the very instant she heard the muazzin call out, "Hayya 'alas salaah!", she would cease whatever she was doing and prepare for salaah.

Similarly, despite her busy schedule, she made time for the 'ibaadah of Allah Ta'ala. Every morning, after performing the Fajr Salaah, she would cover her face with her scarf and engage in the zikr of Allah Ta'ala. Such was her punctuality on her zikr that she would never miss it under any circumstance.

Likewise, for a period of two years, she made the time every day to benefit from her grandson who was becoming an 'Aalim. Her grandson, Qari Muhammad Tayyib (rahimahullah), says, "When I commenced my studies of hadeeth, I would come home every day, after my lessons, and explain the entire lesson to my grandmother. She would listen to the hadeeth with tears flowing from her eyes for the entire duration. This continued for two years."

(Sawaanih-e-Qaasimi vol. 1, pg. 519 and Moulana Muhammad Qaasim Naanotwi – Hayaat aur Kaarnaame pg. 226)

Lessons:

In today's fast-paced world, everybody complains that they 'don't have time'. However, if they regard something to be sufficiently important, they will take out the time for it. Whether it is a waleemah, a chat with a relative or a casual visit to some friend, they will somehow juggle their schedule and find a way to make it fit. Essentially, it all boils down to priorities. Since the respected wife of Moulana Qaasim (rahimahullah) regarded 'ibaadah and Deen to be a priority, she made her schedule fit around this priority. She did not compromise on her salaah or zikr to make time for other engagements and activities.

❀   It is a sign of true imaan that when the Quraan Majeed is recited or the ahaadeeth of Rasulullah (sallallahu 'alaihi wasallam) are read, a person's heart is affected and responds. Such a person will even be moved to the point where tears begin to flow from his eyes due to the softness of his heart.

❀   No matter our age, we are never too old to learn Deen. We should also not regard it as being below our dignity to acquire the necessary knowledge of Deen from a person who is younger than us, just as the wife of Moulana Qaasim (rahimahullah) was learning Deen from her grandson. In fact, this is the blessing of having children and grandchildren who are 'Ulama in one's home – through them, the entire household benefits.

From Luxury to Simplicity

The wife of Moulana Qaasim (rahimahullah) hailed from the village of Deoband. Her father, Shaikh Karaamat Husain, was a wealthy man, and hence on the occasion of her nikaah, when she departed for her husband's home, her father sent her off with an abundance of clothing, expensive jewellery and many household items.

On the first night, Moulana Qaasim (rahimahullah) addressed her saying, "Now that Allah Ta'ala has joined us in marriage, there will have to be compatibility between us. However, in our present condition, this will be difficult, as you are wealthy and I am a pauper. We thus have one of two options; either I become wealthy, which is obviously difficult, or you become poor like me, since this is easy."

Without any hesitation or reservation, she wholeheartedly responded, "I give you the full right to do with my belongings as you please." Accordingly, the very next morning, Moulana (rahimahullah) contributed all her jewellery and wealth in the path of Allah Ta'ala.

Some time thereafter, when she visited her parent's home, her father noticed that she was not wearing any jewellery. When he asked her the reason, she explained to him what had transpired. Despite not saying anything, he felt it inappropriate for his daughter to appear before her relatives dressed in this manner. Being very wealthy, he replaced all her wealth and jewellery once more.

When she returned home, Moulana Qaasim (rahimahullah) observed that she had returned with everything once again. That night, he again encouraged her to prepare for the Hereafter by spending this wealth in the path of Allah Ta'ala. Once again, she gave him the right to do with her wealth as he wished. Thus, the next morning, he gave all her valuables in the path of Allah Ta'ala once again.

The wife of Moulana Qaasim (rahimahullah) would often say, "The love for wealth and jewellery thereafter totally left my heart, and in fact, I even developed an aversion to these things. During my entire life thereafter, I never bought jewellery, nor had a desire for expensive garments."

(Sawaanih-e-Qaasimi vol. 1, pgs. 507-513)

Lessons:

❀ Having hailed from a wealthy home, and having grown up in the lap of luxury, it would not have been easy for the wife of Moulana Qaasim (rahimahullah) to give away her wealth, belongings and jewellery. **Furthermore, many women would be worried about what their relatives, friends and society in general would say about them after their standard of living has been lowered.** However, she understood that obedience to the husband is of paramount importance – especially in the case where her husband was exhorting her to follow the sunnah of simplicity. Hence, she wholeheartedly submitted and sacrificed her wealth.

❀ As far as possible, the in-laws should avoid interfering in the affairs of their married children. When the father of Moulana's (rahimahullah) wife saw that she was dressed in a simple manner, he did not confront Moulana (rahimahullah) nor take him to task. He accepted that since his daughter was the wife of Moulana (rahimahullah), she should try to please him and conform to his wishes.

❁ The love of wealth is a sickness that will plague one until one's death. In this sickness, one will hanker after more and more, with one's appetite never becoming satiated. It is only through adopting the sunnah lifestyle of simplicity that one will gain true happiness in the heart and feel true satisfaction.

A Submissive Spouse

The respected wife of Moulana Qaasim Naanotwi (rahimahullah) was not only a saintly soul – she was also a faithful wife who displayed true loyalty to her husband and went beyond the call of duty in fulfilling his rights.

As the piety, knowledge and wisdom of Moulana Qaasim (rahimahullah) became well known, people from far and wide began to flock to him. As a result, there were always guests in his home, with barely a single meal passing without guests being present. His respected wife was extremely efficient in seeing to the household responsibilities and would ensure that there was always food prepared for the guests. Even when there was a shortage of wealth in the home, she would try her best to honour the guests and see to their comfort. With regard to her big-heartedness, Moulana Qaasim (rahimahullah) once mentioned,

"Our generosity is on account of Ahmad's mother (referring to his respected wife)."

Similarly, she understood the importance of pleasing her husband and was thus completely selfless in her effort to secure his happiness. The following incident, which she herself narrates, is ample evidence in this regard:

"My husband (Moulana Qaasim [rahimahullah]) would generally drink milk at night. Hence, when he returned home after 'Esha, I would present the milk to him. After drinking the milk, he would stand and engage in nafl salaah, as it was his habit to stand in salaah the entire night. If on any occasion he did not wait for me to bring the milk and commenced his salaah, I understood that he was upset with me for some reason. Thus, on the few occasions when he did not wait for the milk and commenced his salaah, I too remained standing the entire night with the cup of milk in my hands."

(*Sawaanih-e-Qaasimi vol.1, pg. 518, Moulana Muhammad Qaasim Naanotwi – Hayaat aur Kaarnaame pgs. 242-245 and Qaasimul 'Uloom Hazrat Moulana Muhammad Qaasim Naanotwi pg. 194*)

Lessons:

- Generosity and big-heartedness are qualities of a true believer. We should always keep our homes open to guests and should try to honour the guests to the best of our ability while keeping within our means. Today, every home has a refrigerator, freezer and microwave, so it is easily possible for a person to keep some food prepared for the unexpected guest. In the case of Moulana Qaasim Naanotwi (rahimahullah), these appliances did not exist. Hence, his wife would have had to prepare food on a daily basis –not just for her own household but for all the guests as well. However, her generosity was such that not only did she do it happily, but she always laid out the best that she could for the guests.

❀ In order for a person to succeed in this life and the next, he will have to fulfil not only the rights of Allah Ta'ala but the rights of the creation as well. In the case of a woman, it is her husband who has the greatest rights over her. The wife of Moulana Qaasim Naanotwi (rahimahullah) understood this, and thus when her husband was displeased with her, even though she did not know the reason for his displeasure, she remained standing the entire night. This was a remarkable demonstration of her selflessness and complete lack of ego and pride.

Going the Extra Mile

The respected wife of Moulana Qaasim Naanotwi (rahimahullah) was blessed with a heart of such compassion and love, that let alone serving her husband she even went the extra mile in serving her mother-in-law and seeing to her comfort.

Shortly before her mother-in-law passed away, she fell ill and would experience bouts of diarrhoea which were so severe that she would soil three or four sets of clothing daily. Together with rendering all the other services, the wife of Moulana Qaasim (rahimahullah) would happily wash the soiled clothing of her mother-in-law. However, Moulana Qaasim (rahimahullah) would also insist on personally washing his mother's clothing. Hence, Moulana Qaasim (rahimahullah) and his wife came to an agreement where they would take turns to wash the clothing.

Despite this arrangement, the wife of Moulana Qaasim (rahimahullah) had such a heart that she would wash, clean and dry the soiled clothing when it was her turn – and when it was her husband's turn as well! However, since her husband wanted to share in the reward of washing his mother's clothing, she would leave just one garment for him to wash.

(Sawaanih-e-Qaasimi vol. 1, pg. 502)

Lessons:

❀ Let alone the soiled clothing of another person, if a person has to soil even his own clothing, he would prefer to give it to a worker to wash rather than washing it himself. However, in the case of Moulana Qaasim (rahimahullah) and his respected wife, they understood the immense reward of serving Moulana's (rahimahullah) mother and regarded it to be their good fortune – not a burden. Hence, Moulana (rahimahullah) wished to earn the reward of serving his mother, while his respected wife also wished to gain the reward. Such was their eagerness that they had to eventually reach a compromise. Sadly, in many homes today, we have the opposite situation. There is an aged father or mother, and it is heart-breaking to see that none of their children want to be 'burdened' with them. Eventually, the children try to reach a compromise so that they can 'share' the burden and minimize the amount that each one is 'lumped' with his parent (may Allah Ta'ala save us!).

❀ The excellence of Moulana Qaasim's (rahimahullah) wife can be understood by the fact that although her husband had excused her from this task, she still insisted on attending to it herself. Furthermore, the person for whom she went the extra mile was not even her own mother – it was her mother-in-law! In this regard, we should always bear in mind that although the mother-in-law is not our own mother, she is our husband's mother. Hence, any friction or unpleasantness with the mother-in-law will most definitely have a negative impact on the marriage, as it will displease the husband. Thus, in the interest of our marriages, and to uphold the sunnah of showing good character and serving people (even when they ill-treat us), we should try, to the best of our ability, to serve our mothers-in-law and be good to them.

Mother of Moulana 'Umar Paalanpuri (rahimahullah)

Moulded by His Mother

Moulana Muhammad 'Umar Paalanpuri (rahimahullah) was an illustrious scholar and renowned daa'ee (preacher) who was born in the year 1929. His passion for the effort of da'wat and tableegh (an effort to rekindle the spirit of imaan in Muslims) was such that he made no less than eighty-one journeys to foreign countries for the propagation of Deen. Over and above this, Allah Ta'ala had blessed him to perform hajj twenty times.

Allah Ta'ala had blessed him with a captivating manner of oration. Hence, he would deliver lectures before tens of thousands of people. Through his lectures, multitudes would be inspired to repent from their wrongs and change the direction of their lives, and they would resolve to sacrifice their wealth, time and lives for the cause of Allah's Deen.

When Moulana Muhammad 'Umar Paalanpuri (rahimahullah) was just eight years old, his father, Wazeerud Deen, passed away, leaving him an orphan to be raised by his mother. However, his mother was a very pious woman. Hence, Moulana (rahimahumullah) mentioned that some of his earliest memories, from his childhood, were of his mother performing salaah and weeping before Allah Ta'ala in du'aa.

Together with her piety, Allah Ta'ala had inspired her to raise her son in such a remarkable manner that she can be attributed with moulding him into the man that he became.

Such was her constant concern and commitment to raising her children correctly that she remained watchful at all times, observing their behaviour. When she would bring anything home for her children to enjoy, she would give it to them and instruct them to share it among themselves. She would then observe them to see who displayed signs of greediness or generosity, and she would accordingly correct them and address their weakness.

(Sawaanih Moulana Muhammad 'Umar Paalanpuri [rahimahullah] pg. 59 and Mithaali Khawaateen pg. 270)

Hereunder we will discuss various inspirational aspects from this great woman's life.

Lessons:

❦ "First impressions are lasting impressions". When the earliest memories of Moulana Paalanpuri (rahimahullah) were of his mother performing salaah and weeping in du'aa, we can well imagine the indelible impression it created on his young, innocent mind! **Conversely, if a child is raised in an environment of music, movies, loose morals and un-Islamic behaviour,** then the resulting ill-effect on the child is obvious.

❀   If we want our child to become a pious Muslim, **then we will have to start with developing our own piety,** as one cannot pass on that which one himself does not possess.

❀   Raising a child correctly is a constant occupation. At no time can the parents 'take a break', **as the child, at every moment, is undergoing some experience that is shaping who he will ultimately become in life.**

Shaping the Mindset

The mother of Moulana Muhammad 'Umar Paalanpuri (rahimahullah) was a simple, uneducated woman. However, despite her lack of education, she had tremendous zeal and enthusiasm for Deen.

In their neighborhood, there was a pious and learned woman known as Maryam Khaalah (Aunt Maryam). The mother of Moulana (rahimahullah) would frequent this woman to learn the aspects of Deen and imaan. Due to her spending time in the company of Maryam Khaalah, her fear of Allah Ta'ala and concern for the Hereafter increased.

The mother of Moulana (rahimahullah) also made an effort to instill these same qualities into her son. Hence, Moulana (rahimahullah) would say, "I may have taught the Quraan Majeed to my mother, but it was my mother who set me on the path of the Quraan Majeed."

Moulana (rahimahullah) explains: "My mother ensured that we spoke of something relating to Deen and imaan on a daily basis. Hence, since my childhood, my mother would tell me the incidents of the various Ambiyaa ('alaihimus salaam) mentioned in the Quraan Majeed, as well as those things that would instil within me the fear of Allah Ta'ala and Qiyaamah. She would say, 'Son! Read the incident of Nabi Yusuf ('alaihis salaam) from the book today!' Likewise, on other nights, I would read the incident of Nabi Moosa ('alaihis salaam) or Nabi 'Isa ('alaihis salaam). Being a small child, my attention would sometimes drift and I would run off. However, in order to mould my mindset, she would call me back and we would continue."

On account of Moulana's (rahimahullah) tender age, when his mother would explain some concept of Deen to him, it would become firmly entrenched in his heart and mind.

Moulana (rahimahullah) mentions: "Once, my mother described the scenes of Qiyaamah to me, telling me how the sky will crack, the earth will shake, etc. That night, when I went to sleep, I began to dream of the scenes of Qiyaamah. Coincidentally, while I was asleep and having this dream, my younger brother fell off his bed and landed on me. This gave me such a fright that I began to yell and shout, 'Qiyaamah has come! I will have to account for my actions!' My mother lit the lamp and asked, "'Umar! Why are you crying? Nothing happened. Your brother just fell on you!' However, I kept my eyes tightly shut and continued to cry saying, 'Qiyaamah has come!'"

(Sawaanih Moulana Muhammad 'Umar Paalanpuri (rahimahullah) pg. 59 and Mithaali Khawaateen pg. 271)

Lessons:

❀ The mother of Moulana (rahimahullah) had true zeal for Deen. Hence, she identified the woman in her locality who was pious and would frequent her company in order to strengthen her imaan. This teaches us the value and importance of good company. Through the blessing of Maryam Khaalah's company, not only did Moulana's (rahimahullah) mother benefit, but the positive effects rubbed off onto Moulana (rahimahullah) himself as well. Hence, we should all try to find good company for ourselves – company that will remind us of Allah Ta'ala and will strengthen our imaan.

❀ A child is young, highly impressionable and easily influenced. Hence, the lessons taught to a child and values instilled into his heart at a young age generally remain with him for life. However, for these lessons to take root and become entrenched, they will need to be regularly repeated. It is for this reason that the mother of Moulana (rahimahullah) would conduct ta'leem on a daily basis and narrate the stories of the Ambiyaa ('alaihimus salaam) to her son.

Instilling Qualities of Imaan

The mother of Moulana Muhammad 'Umar Paalanpuri (rahimahullah) paid special attention to his upbringing and made a continuous effort to instil qualities of piety within him. Hence, she would regularly advise him and teach him important Islamic values.

On one occasion, she mentioned to her son, "When you are placed in the grave, two angels will come to you, and they will ask you three questions." She then explained the three questions, together with the answers, to her son. Thereafter, on another occasion, when she began to speak to him and caution him regarding the punishment in the grave, he responded, "I have already learnt the questions of the angels and the answers to their questions (so I do not need to worry about punishment in the grave)." Hearing this, she replied, "When you are in the grave, it will not be your tongue of flesh that will speak – it will be the tongue of your actions that will speak (i.e. you will only be able to give the correct answers if your actions and beliefs were in order)."

On another occasion, she advised him saying, "O my son! If you wish to make gheebah of (backbite) any person, then make my gheebah so that your good deeds will at least remain in the home. The reason is that through making my gheebah, your good deeds will be given to me (and if you are going to give your deeds to anyone, at least give them to me)." In giving her son this advice, she did not literally mean that he should engage in backbiting and speak ill of her. Rather, her intention was to instil in his heart the seriousness and danger of this sin.

Once, a certain house was sold in the neighbourhood. On learning that a house was sold, Moulana's (rahimahullah) mother asked him, "Whose house was sold?" In reply, Moulana (rahimahullah) used the words, "The maalik (owner) of the house is so-and-so." The moment these words left his mouth, she became upset and reprimanded him saying, "Allah alone is the Maalik (the true owner of everything)! Why did you refer to that person as being the maalik of the house!" Eventually, Moulana (rahimahullah) asked Maryam Khaalah to intercede to his mother on his behalf, and it was only then that her anger subsided.

(Sawaanih Moulana Muhammad 'Umar Paalanpuri pgs. 60 & 68)

Lessons:

❀ It is often said that a child's first madrasah is his mother's lap. This can be clearly seen in the upbringing of Moulana Muhammad 'Umar Paalanpuri (rahimahullah), as his mother continued to entrench the values of imaan and Islam into his heart throughout his childhood, **paving the path for his future progress and success.**

❁   Though what Moulana (rahimahullah) said was not wrong, when he referred to the owner as the 'maalik', his mother was so conscious of Allah Ta'ala that she could not tolerate anyone else being referred to as Maalik. Nevertheless, her conducting in this manner left such an impression on his mind that he would have always been cognisant of Allah Ta'ala being the true Owner of everything, and this belief would have been cemented into his mind.

Making Her Dream a Reality

It had always been the aspiration and desire of the mother of Moulana Muhammad 'Umar Paalanpuri (rahimahullah) that her son become an 'Aalim of Deen, and Allah Ta'ala made this dream of her's a reality.

Maryam Khaalah had once narrated the hadeeth to her which mentions that the parents of the haafiz of the Quraan Majeed will be honoured by being made to wear crowns of noor on the Day of Qiyaamah. Hearing this hadeeth, his mother began to weep and said to her son, "My son! I want you to learn the Quraan Majeed, and you must learn Saheeh Bukhaari as well!" Moulana (rahimahullah) asked, "What will happen to my school education?" His mother replied, "That is not my concern – my only concern is that you acquire the knowledge of Deen!"

At the age of seven, Moulana (rahimahullah) enrolled into a school in Bombay. It was the following year, when he was eight years old, that his father passed away. Moulana (rahimahullah) remained in school for five years, until the year 1942, when he returned with his mother to spend the holiday in his hometown. While he was at home during the holiday, his mother began sending him to the local madrasah in which a very pious 'Aalim, Moulana 'Abdul Hafeez Jalaalpuri (rahimahullah), was teaching. Moulana 'Abdul Hafeez (rahimahullah) showed him special attention, and under his tutelage, Moulana progressed tremendously, studying no less than fifty kitaabs in one year.

During the course of this year, Moulana 'Abdul Hafeez (rahimahullah) needed to return to his hometown in the province of U.P., over a thousand kilometers away. He sent a message to Moulana's (rahimahullah) mother saying, "I want to take your son with me to my hometown so that his studies will not suffer (and I can continue to teach him)." Moulana's (rahimahullah) mother was determined to make her son an 'Aalim, so she acquired a loan of fifty rupees due to her financial contraints, and sent him to study Deen.

When Moulana's (rahimahullah) mother initially took the decision to send him to madrasah to become an 'Aalim, her relatives from Bombay came to her and attempted to convince her to keep him in school, especially as he was excelling and had achieved remarkable grades. They even said to her, "What will become of him when he is a Moulana? If you do not give him school education, how will he earn a livelihood? **He will even be dependent on people for his roti!**" To this, his mother replied, "If he studies Deen correctly, then Allah Ta'ala will cause the world to fall at his feet."

Moulana (rahimahullah) was once reading to his mother from a certain book when she spontaneously said, "O my son! Today, you are reading to me and only I am listening to you! Allah Ta'ala will bring the day when hundreds of thousands of people will listen to you! I have no doubt regarding this!"

(Sawaanih Moulana Muhammad 'Umar Paalanpuri (rahimahullah) pgs. 59-63 and Mithaali Khawaateen pgs. 271-273)

Lessons:

Every parent has aspirations and dreams for their child, and they are prepared to make any sacrifice for their child's sake. Moulana's (rahimahullah) mother was no different – however her dream was for her son to become an 'Aalim of Deen, serving Islam and spreading the message of Allah Ta'ala. **For this purpose, she was even prepared to send her young son over a thousand kilometres away with his ustaaz, and even took a loan to fund his studies.**

When faced with the opposition of her family, Moulana's (rahimahullah) mother stood firm. **She explained that if her son** studied Deen correctly (i.e. he works with dedication and studies solely for the sake of pleasing Allah Ta'ala – not for any other motive), then Allah Ta'ala will most certainly look after him. In fact, the words that she used were 'the world will fall at his feet' – and this became a reality.

Moulana's (rahimahullah) mother wanted him to become an 'Aalim so that he would become her investment in the Hereafter, and so that he could help her to improve her Deen. Hence, although he was the son and she was the mother, she would ask him to teach her and educate her regarding different aspects of Deen. This clearly highlights the level of her sincerity and her zeal for Deen.

The Fruit of Her Effort

The mother of Moulana Muhammad 'Umar Paalanpuri (rahimahullah) considered no sacrifice too small in the path of her son becoming an 'Aalim of Deen.

At the time when he was leaving for Darul 'Uloom Deoband for the final year of his studies, she was weak and suffering ill health. She was unable to see, could barely chew and could not walk. However, despite her ailing condition, she sacrificed her son's companionship and service, giving preference to Deen and sending him to madrasah. At the time of his departure, she lovingly passed her hand over his head and said to him, "Go, my son!"

Thereafter, while Moulana (rahimahullah) was over a thousand kilometers away, completing his studies, his mother's condition deteriorated. Understanding that her demise was imminent, her family members suggested to her, "Should we send a message and call Muhammad 'Umar from Deoband?" She replied, "No! No! He has gone for the sake of Deen! I have no good deeds to my account – he is the only asset that I have for the Hereafter!" She then said, "If Allah Ta'ala has to ask me, 'What good have you brought?' I will reply, 'I have left my son in the path of Your Deen and come to You. I only sacrificed the companionship of my son for Your sake!'"

As her final moment drew near, she remarked, "I can perceive a beautiful fragrance!" This was despite the fact that her sense of smell and other senses had ceased to function some time previously. Thereafter, she made salaam, smiled and fell unconscious. On regaining consciousness, her family asked her, "To whom did you make salaam, and what caused you to smile?" She replied, "I saw my son, Muhammad 'Umar, between two angels. He made salaam to me (and I replied to his salaam), and seeing my son caused me to smile."

It was on that day, 14th December 1955, that this inspirational woman breathed her last and departed from this world.

After her demise, Moulana (rahimahullah) saw her in a dream and asked her, "Mother! Where are you?" She replied in Arabic (whereas she could not speak Arabic during her lifetime), "Ana fil Jannah (I am in Jannah)." She then said to Moulana (rahimahullah), "You did not get the opportunity to take me for hajj." Hence, Moulana (rahimahullah) thereafter performed hajj and conveyed the reward of the hajj to his mother.

(Sawaanih Moulana Muhammad 'Umar Paalanpuri (rahimahullah) pg. 67 and Mithaali Khawaateen pg. 273)

Lessons:

❀ Generally, a person will believe in that which he can see. However, imaan is based on us believing in the unseen. The mother of Moulana (rahimahullah) had firm imaan and unshakeable conviction in the promises of Allah Ta'ala and Rasulullah (sallallahu 'alaihi wasallam). Hence, she ensured that she made him an 'Aalim, as she had hope that Allah Ta'ala would reward her for dedicating her son to the service of Deen. This conviction was well rewarded, as Allah Ta'ala accepted her son for Deen and made him the means of thousands of people reforming their lives.

❀ The mother of Moulana (rahimahullah) may have been uneducated, but her heart was filled with enthusiasm and zeal for Deen. Hence, purely for the sake of Deen, she was prepared to sacrifice the companionship of her beloved son during the stage of her life when she required it the most. It was this quality, of always giving preference to the Deen of Allah Ta'ala, that stood out in the life of this great woman.

Mother of Moulana Abul Hasan 'Ali Nadwi (rahimahullah)

An Exemplary Mother

Moulana Sayyid Abul Hasan 'Ali Nadwi (rahimahullah) was an internationally renowned 'Aalim of the recent past, who was well known for his mastery in the Arabic language, despite hailing from the land of India. His proficiency in Arabic was such that he authored many books in Arabic which received fame and acclaim in the Arab and non-Arab world. In fact, many of his Arabic books are studied in madaaris and universities world-wide as elementary text books for learning the Arabic language.

Together with his command of Arabic, Moulana's (rahimahullah) other field of specialty was history – specifically studying the rise and fall of nations and the factors that led to their decline.

Moulana (rahimahullah) was also actively involved in the effort of da'wat and tableegh and delivered talks in many ijtimaas. Furthermore, he played a major role in introducing the work of da'wat to the Arab countries. Allah Ta'ala had granted Moulana (rahimahullah) international acceptance as he travelled to almost all the Muslim countries, from Malaysia in the east to Morocco in the west, and to many non-Muslim countries as well, conveying the message of Deen.

Moulana (rahimahullah) passed away on the Day of Jumu'ah, 22 Ramadhaan 1420 A.H. (31 December 1999). Janaazah Salaah in absentia was performed in the Harams of Makkah Mukarramah and Madeenah Munawwarah (which is permissible according to the Shaafi'ee and Hambali mazhab). It is thus estimated that 3.5 million people performed his janaazah salaah in the Harams alone.

As Moulana's (rahimahullah) father had passed away when he was still a young child, it was Moulana's (rahimahullah) mother who saw to his upbringing and single-handedly raised him. She was undoubtedly an exceptional mother to have raised such an exceptional son. The fruits of her efforts are evident in the success and acceptance which Allah Ta'ala granted Moulana (rahimahullah).

Being a prolific writer, Moulana (rahimahullah) wrote a detailed biography of his mother entitled "Zikr-e-Khair" which will soon be published in English by Uswatul Muslimah, insha-Allah. Hereunder are a few important and relevant incidents from this biography so that we can learn from the life of this exemplary woman.

Lesson:

❦ Every child is raised under the influence of one or more people who serve to mould the child into the man he will one day become. In the case of Moulana Abul Hasan (rahimahullah), it was his mother, with her unique approach to raising him, who moulded him into the internationally accepted 'Aalim that he became. Hence, everything that Allah Ta'ala blessed him to achieve is actually a reflection of her perfection. Therefore, if parents wish for their child to be blessed with piety and serve the Deen of Allah Ta'ala, the parent will first have to make changes in their own lives, as only then will they be able to suitably influence their child.

The Environment of Righteousness

The mother of Moulana Abul Hasan (rahimahullah) was born in 1296 A.H. (1878) and was appropriately named "Khairun Nisaa" – the best of women.

She was blessed with a very pious father whose piety and saintliness rubbed off on her. In fact, the signs of piety were already evident in her from a young age. When her father would awaken at the time of Tahajjud Salaah and descend from the upper story of their home to proceed to the masjid, her eyes would open and she too would awake. Then she, together with her middle sister, Saalihah, would ascend to the upper story where they would engage in performing nafl salaah with their mother.

Another factor that contributed to her upbringing and helped to instil noble qualities in her was a special practice they upheld in their home, which was common in many other homes of the past as well. Her son, Moulana (rahimahullah), writes regarding this system:

"In those days, it was a common practice among prominent families for women who were widows or old, and either had nobody to care for them or wished to devote the remainder of their lives to the worship of Allah Ta'ala, to leave their homes and settle into the homes of their relatives. They would thereafter spend the remainder of their lives with respect, engaging in the zikr of Allah Ta'ala and preparing for the Hereafter.

In our family, almost every home had such a woman who would live there for some years. The home of my nana (maternal grandfather) and his brother were among the most prominent and well to-do homes and it was their home that housed the greatest number of these old women, the majority of whom were either bay'at (a pledge to follow the teachings of the spiritual mentor for one's self-reformation) to my nana or some other saint of the family.

These women had very firm imaan, were very particular regarding their time and were sources of immense barakah and blessings. Their presence in the homes enhanced the Deeni discussions and activities of the home and had a very positive influence on the young girls of the family."

Lessons:

🌸 The habits and ways that are instilled into a person during their childhood generally remain with them throughout their life as these are their formative years which pave the way to their future progress. **Similarly, what a child observes and experiences serves to mould the mindset and outlook of the child. Thus, when a child receives an upbringing of this nature, where her very first sight, on awakening, is that of her father proceeding for salaah, and her first action on awakening is to perform Tahajjud Salaah, we can well imagine the piety of that child later in life.**

🌸 **How unfortunate it is that today, let alone other elderly women,** even our own parents and grandparents are not welcome in our homes and are thrown into old-age homes! **These old people should not be viewed as burdens to be offloaded elsewhere. The reality of the matter is that serving these old people, caring for them and seeing to their comfort, with love and respect, is the means for immense barakah (blessings) to enter the home and to secure the special mercy of Allah Ta'ala. While this system, of caring for the old, was once a common practice, it has sadly become near-extinct. Hence, instead of the children in the home being taught the quality of compassion and to care for the weak, they are taught to be selfish and self-centred, and to place their comforts before the needs of anyone else.

Carefully Controlled Education

The mother of Moulana Abul Hasan (rahimahullah), Khairun Nisaa (rahimahallah), was raised in a family in which the education of the womenfolk was very carefully controlled and was not allowed to exceed a certain level. In this regard, reading, writing and education beyond the basics were not approved of for the women of the family. Rather, their education would be limited to learning the relevant, necessary masaa-il of Deen and matters which would assist them in running a home and attending to domestic affairs. Additionally, the kitaabs (books) of such 'Ulama in whom the family felt confidence were, to some degree, included in the syllabus.

In fact, for the girls of the family, learning to write was actually discouraged to some extent, and some of the pious elders of the family were very strict in this regard. They would explain their stance and motive saying, "If girls learn to write, they may begin writing to strange men." However, due to the outstanding piety of Khairun Nisaa (rahimahallah), a special concession was made for her to learn to write. She was thereafter blessed by Allah Ta'ala to use this talent of hers in a very noble cause – to author beneficial and excellent books.

While strict control was exercised regarding education and writing, certain skills and talents which are prized within a woman were encouraged and imparted to them at a very advanced level. One of these skills is the ability to sew. Khairun Nisaa (rahimahallah) had an inherent talent for sewing and embroidery. In fact, she was so skilled that her sewing seemed to be that of a professional seamstress, and such was her flair that she would regularly create new styles and designs.

Lessons:

❁ **For a woman to become pious, it is not necessary that she remain illiterate.** Rather, what is necessary is that we recognize the dangers of literacy and modern education and put measures into place that will save ourselves and our progenies from falling prey to them. A simple example is that of novels. How many young girls have had a complete summersault in their thinking and behaviour after reading certain novels? Likewise, how many girls have fallen into an illicit relationship or bad company via WhatsApp, Instagram or other similar communication platforms? All these ills and harms stem from the lack of careful monitoring and control by the parents who wish to empower their children, but fail to recognize the associated dangers.

🌹   If a woman is a talented seamstress, she will be good for herself and good for others as well. If the need ever arises, she will even be able to earn a livelihood with respect from the confines of her home. Furthermore, she will be occupied and productive and will never be driven by boredom to occupy herself in activities that are harmful to her Deen and imaan.

The First Haafizah

Among the many unique qualities of Khairun Nisaa (rahimahallah) was that she was an excellent haafizah and remained dedicated to the Quraan Majeed until the end of her life.

Memorizing the Quraan Majeed was common among the males of her family, and the family had produced many outstanding huffaaz. However, among the women, there was nobody who had memorized the Quraan Majeed, until Khairun Nisaa (rahimahallah).

She was the first woman of the family who made the intention to memorize the Quraan Majeed. Thereafter, other females in the family also developed the enthusiasm and zeal to do hifz. Thus, she, together with her middle sister, Saalihah, her niece and two other cousins all commenced memorizing the Quraan Majeed together.

In doing so, they had requested their brothers or some other mahram of the family to assist them and supervise their memorization. Khairun Nisaa's (rahimahallah) youngest brother,

Sayyid 'Ubaidullah, was an excellent haafiz and would recite the Quraan Majeed both correctly and beautifully. Khairun Nisaa (rahimahallah) thus memorized the Quraan Majeed under his supervision, completing her hifz in approximately three years.

Moulana (rahimahullah) writes: "They all recited the Quraan Majeed excellently and their tajweed was extremely refined. If it was not for the fear of disrespect, I would venture as far as to say that they even recited better than many of those who graduate from madrasahs today. The enthusiasm and naturally beautiful tone with which they recited only served to further enhance their recitation. I remember once coming to discreetly listen to my mother recite the Quraan Majeed. (Such was the tranquillity and peace experienced that) it seemed as if rain was falling gently from the sky, and until today, I still remember the enjoyment I derived from listening to her recitation."

Her commitment to her hifz was such that even after her marriage, she would recite her dhor (revision of the Quraan Majeed) to her husband. Thereafter, from the time of his demise until the end of her life, she continued to recite to her nephew, Haafiz Sayyid Habeebur Rahmaan, so long as her memory served her.

Lessons:

❀ There is great virtue and reward for a person who memorizes the Quraan Majeed. However, it is a lifelong commitment and responsibility. Furthermore, the sin for neglecting and forgetting the Quraan Majeed after memorizing it is very severe. It should not be that a girl memorizes the Quraan Majeed in her youth and thereafter neglects doing dhor (revision) or reciting it after marriage and thus forgets it.

It was for this very reason that despite wishing for her daughter to become a haafizah, Khairun Nisaa (rahimahallah) advised her against continuing with her hifz after commencing it and completing six paras (juz). She explained the reason to her saying, "There is nobody to listen to your dhor (revision), so it will be very difficult for you to revise and retain what you have memorized."

❀ Khairun Nisaa (rahimahallah) and the other females in her family who memorized the Quraan Majeed, did so under the supervision of their mahrams and from the safety of their homes. In other words, they maintained the highest levels of hayaa, hijaab and niqaab when acquiring the knowledge of Deen. In stark contrast to that is the trend today where women attend lessons delivered by male scholars without the basic law of hijaab and niqaab being observed.

❀ Recitation of the Quraan Majeed is an action which enlivens a home, draws the mercy of Allah Ta'ala and barakah, and attracts the Angels. It is thus important that we recite the Quraan Majeed within our homes on a daily basis. Together with reciting, we should make an effort to ensure that we are reciting correctly. If we have not learnt to recite correctly, let us approach someone who recites correctly and ask them to assist and teach us. We are never too old to apply ourselves to perfecting our recitation of the

Quraan Majeed. How embarrassing it is when a child asks the mother to assist them in their madrasah sabaq (lesson) to which the mother has to reply that she herself is unable to read!

A Husband of Deen or Dunya?

When Khairun Nisaa (rahimahallah) came of marriageable age, the family of her paternal uncle was making every effort to secure her proposal to her cousin. Two of her sisters were already married into their household and their home was one of affluence and prosperity. Thus, from the perspective of financial security, there was no better home than her paternal uncle's home, and living under his roof would guarantee that she enjoyed a grand and comfortable lifestyle.

Due to these reasons, both Khairun Nisaa (rahimahallah) and her mother were inclined to accepting this proposal. Her father, however, wanted her husband to be a pious and Allah-fearing person, and this quality of piety was not found in his brother's home to a level that satisfied him. In other words, they had abundant wealth and many properties, but there was no real spirit and environment of Deen in their home.

Therefore, when she received a proposal from Moulana Sayyid Hakeem 'Abdul Hayy (rahimahullah), then although he had been married previously (his wife had passed away), her father was excited and felt as if the proposal he had desired all along had finally arrived.

Since the proposal came from a household that was not concerned about wealth, and furthermore, they were undergoing a period of difficulty and constraint, her mother was very worried and reluctant to accept the proposal. Her father, however, was determined and said, "Sayyid is young, pious, an 'Aalim and intelligent. I cannot give preference to anyone else over him. Wealth and poverty have no importance in my eyes. The factor by which we must decide is piety and the knowledge of Deen."

During this period of deliberation and uncertainty, Khairun Nisaa (rahimahallah) saw multiple dreams which indicated that her marriage to him would be a means of Allah Ta'ala blessing her with special favours and bounties. Hence, accepting the advice of her father, she accepted the proposal and her nikaah was performed to Moulana Sayyid Hakeem 'Abdul Hayy (rahimahullah).

Lessons:

❁ When either we or our children approach marriageable age, it is only natural that we begin to look for a prospective partner. However, when looking for a partner, what are the criteria based on which we assess, judge and compare proposals? Many of us largely base our decision on the financial strength of the person as we have concern for our material security and comfort. While this is not impermissible, it should not be the main basis for our decision, **as Rasulullah (sallallahu 'alaihi wasallam) encouraged us to base our decision on the person's commitment to Deen.** While there is no guarantee that securing wealth will ensure comfort in this world, *securing Deen will definitely secure comfort in this world and the Hereafter.* How many women, married to wealthy men, face unhappy marriages and although seem to 'have it all', are secretly miserable? If the decision is made on the basis of taqwa (the consciousness of Allah Ta'ala), the spouse will never ill-treat you as he has the fear of Allah Ta'ala.

❁ **In the modern world of today, many young people find and choose their spouse on their own. Often, when they mention their choice to their parents, then their parents, in their wisdom, foresight and experience, disapprove as they can clearly see that there is a lack of compatibility.** At this point, the child, blinded by 'love', feels that his parents are trying to 'spite' him, instead of realizing that they know better and wish the best for him. Finding a spouse independently generally involves pre-marital relationships, resulting in the relationship commencing with the displeasure of Allah Ta'ala. On the other hand, pleasing one's parents is an action that will draw barakah (blessings) and the pleasure of Allah Ta'ala. Thus Khairun Nisaa (rahimahallah) pleased her father and accepted to marry Moulana 'Abdul Hayy (rahimahullah).

Making the Marriage

After her marriage, when Khairun Nisaa (rahimahallah) entered her new home, she found that the description which she had always heard regarding the home was indeed true. It was an era of poverty, and if there was food on one day, there would sometimes be hunger the next.

Despite this level poverty, she did not disclose or reveal the situation to anyone. In fact, she went to extremes in concealing the poverty of her in-laws and safeguarding their honour.

Occasionally, her mother would send a maid to her home to see whether there was anything cooking on the stove. However, as soon as she spotted someone approaching, she would hastily place a pot of water on the stove and light the fire. Hence, the visitor would be under the impression that there was food cooking in the home. In this way she concealed the true reality – that there was nothing at home to cook. Nevertheless, her mother would sometimes perceive that there was no food in the home and would pack a tray of food and send it for her daughter.

Shortly after their marriage, her husband decided to open a clinic. Allah Ta'ala made it a success, and the barakah (blessings) that now began to pour into the home was such that the entire home was transformed. With this small income, they were able to achieve what even the wealthy were unable to achieve. All the needs of the home were seen to with extreme comfort and ease. In fact, together with seeing to their own needs, they were even able to see to the needs of others and would frequently entertain guests.

Khairun Nisaa (rahimahallah) herself writes: "This home became like Jannah for me, and the service which I carried out for my in-laws was a great source of Allah Ta'ala's mercy for me. It felt as if I was now under the shade of Allah Ta'ala's mercy. I had no worry or concern, and my every moment was spent in gratitude to Allah Ta'ala."

Lessons:

🌹 In the past, people did not enter a marriage expecting to find it a ready-made heaven. Instead, they understood that what they put into the marriage would be what they got out of it. Hence, they had a mindset of making the marriage and making the home – no matter what adversity they faced or what difficulty they underwent. Thus, in those times, the divorce rate was far lower than today, the homes were fairly stable, and very few children became delinquents.

🌹 If a person safeguards the honour of the next person, Allah Ta'ala will bless him with great honour and respect. Khairun Nisaa (rahimahallah) went beyond the call of duty, even enduring hardship and difficulty, for the sake of safeguarding the honour of her in-laws. As a result, Allah Ta'ala not only blessed her with tremendous honour and respect, but He made her find such happiness in her in-laws' home that she herself referred to it as being "like Jannah".

❀   Khairun Nisaa (rahimahallah) understood that serving her in-laws would please her husband, and win his heart and the heart of his parents. Hence, although it was not compulsory upon her to serve them, she did so anyway. The outcome of her selflessness and humility was that she enjoyed a blissful marriage.

❀   Ultimately, the happy, prosperous marriage that Khairun Nisaa (rahimahallah) enjoyed was on account of her accepting her father's advice and basing her marriage decision primarily on piety. The barakah and blessing that followed was such that Allah Ta'ala not only blessed her with a pious husband, but He also blessed her with wealth and prosperity, thus bestowing her with the best of both, Deen and dunya (material).

Going Above and Beyond

In her role as a wife, Khairun Nisaa (rahimahallah) fulfilled her domestic chores and responsibilities in the most excellent manner, and her entire life reflected her spirit of selflessness and sacrificing for the sake of others.

When serving her husband, she did so with passion and devotion. Hence, although there was a servant employed to prepare meals, she would insist on personally cooking for him, and would go out of her way to serve him exquisite dishes and desserts. In fact, her expertise in the culinary department was such that she was later able to author a best-selling recipe book named 'Zaa-iqah'.

Her husband was a very hospitable person and would bring guests home for meals on a daily basis. Khairun Nisaa (rahimahallah) would always apply herself to the preparations, presenting multiple dishes and sweets to the guests.

Since she was living in Lucknow, which is a city, many of the family children from rural areas were boarding with her for study purposes. She would not only take care of all these children, but would even try to accommodate and cater for their different preferences, tastes, likes and dislikes.

Lessons:

In a relationship of love, it is the 'personal touch' that is valued, prized and enhances the relationship. Hence, when a person loves a certain celebrity, he does not only purchase his autobiography – he tries to get it hand-signed by the author himself. In the same way, Khairun Nisaa (rahimahallah) ensured that she 'hand-signed' and put a 'personal touch' on every meal that her husband enjoyed. Had she wished, she could have relaxed and enjoyed some leisure time while the servant did the work. However, she realized that showing love and devotion to her husband in this manner would please him, and more importantly, it would please Allah Ta'ala. Thus, she went above and beyond in serving her husband.

● Entertaining guests is encouraged in Islam and is a means of drawing immense barakah (blessings) into the home. Furthermore, honouring the guest is greatly emphasized in the ahaadeeth of Rasulullah (sallallahu 'alaihi wasallam). Hence, Khairun Nisaa (rahimahallah) never complained over her husband bringing guests home on a daily basis, but rather served them to the best of her ability, every single day.

● A salient quality of the Sahaabah (radhiyallahu 'anhum) was that they were always prepared to sacrifice their own comfort for others. Khairun Nisaa (rahimahallah) was indeed blessed with this quality – not only in serving her husband's guests but also in caring for the family children boarding with her. Had she wished, she could have told them to stop being fussy, but instead, she took pity on them, sacrificed her own comfort, and tried to cater for each child's individual preferences.

Dealing with the Demise of Her Husband

Life was full of happiness, joy and prosperity for Khairun Nisaa (rahimahallah) when suddenly, the tragedy of her husband's demise struck in 1341 A.H. (1923). As soon as the news of her husband's demise was broken to her, she fell into sajdah in submission before Allah Ta'ala.

After the demise of her husband, she once again experienced numerous difficulties and constraints. Her husband had only left one rupee as cash and he had never owned estates and properties. Whatever was earned was spent that very day.

During her 'iddat and afterwards as well, she remained engaged in mainly two occupations. One was listening to books of Deen being read to her, and the second was the occupation in which she spent most of her life – du'aa and 'ibaadah.

Furthermore, her family had an excellent practice which they implemented in order to keep them motivated whenever a calamity occurred. They would read the incidents of the valour, bravery, pain and sacrifice of the Sahaabah (radhiyallahu 'anhum). When reading these incidents, they would forget their own grief and sorrow and an environment of consolation, patience and submission would be created in the home.

Lessons:

- There are many families and households that have went from prosperity to poverty overnight as a job was lost or some other calamity occurred. In such challenging times, it is easy to collapse into despondency and lose all hope. However, Khairun Nisaa (rahimahallah) immediately turned to Allah Ta'ala, and continued to turn to Him, trusting that He would assist her and take care of her. No matter what problem we may have, we too need to turn to Allah Ta'ala and entrust our affairs to Him, as He is sufficient for us and will never abandon or forget us.

❀ When we regularly read the incidents of the Sahaabah (radhiyallahu 'anhum), it gives us an imaani strength which assists us in remaining firm on Deen and coping with the various challenges that we may face in life. It also provides us with perspective and makes us realize that although our struggles seem major, they are minor when compared to the difficulties faced by the Sahaabah (radhiyallahu 'anhum). This assists us to remain grateful to Allah Ta'ala for all the favours we still enjoy, and also helps us to remain positive and hopeful. A simple way of achieving this is to conduct ta'leem daily in our homes.

Committed to Du'aa and 'Ibaadah

The attachment that Khairun Nisaa (rahimahallah) had with making du'aa was indeed proverbial. Apart from the sunnah du'aas pertaining to different occasions, she would remain almost perpetually engaged in du'aa. It was this favour of Allah Ta'ala upon her (of inspiring her to make abundant du'aa) that became a great means of her progress and opened the door to her enjoying countless special favours and blessings of Allah Ta'ala.

Khairun Nisaa (rahimahallah) herself explained that in her experience, whenever Allah Ta'ala wanted to bless her with something, he would first make her beg for it in du'aa. She would be overcome by a feeling of acute distress and anxiety, and it was only through crying to Allah Ta'ala in du'aa that her heart would once again feel solace and peace.

She had a natural affinity for poetry, and thus, while making du'aa, the words would flow from her lips in the form of poetry. Her love for du'aa was such that she even composed a book named 'Baab-e-Rahmat' – The Door of Mercy, in which she wrote du'aas in the form of poetry.

Together with du'aa, Khairun Nisaa (rahimahallah) was extremely committed to her other ma'moolaat (daily nafl 'ibaadah), such as the recitation of the Quraan Majeed and performance of Tahajjud Salaah.

The time of Tahajjud was the time which she cherished and anticipated the most. Each day, she made an effort to wake up for Tahajjud even earlier than the previous day. Towards the end of her life, on account of her weakness and other ailments, her family members continuously tried to convince her to wake up a little later for Tahajjud. However, she was not prepared to accept their suggestion.

In fact, it was when she had awoken for Tahajjud Salaah and was being led to the bathroom that she fell, breaking her shoulder and wrist due to the darkness and her sleepiness, and it was this incident that caused her final illness to commence.

Lessons:

🌸 Du'aa is not only the means of a believer placing his needs before Allah Ta'ala and getting them fulfilled, but is also a great act of 'ibaadah. How sad it is that we can make up to ten phone calls – if not more – and spend hours standing in a line in order to fulfil our needs, yet we find it difficult to make wudhu, perform two rakaats of salaah and raise our hands, placing our needs before Almighty Allah Ta'ala! A person once mentioned, "The quickest route between a problem and its solution is the distance between the forehead and the musalla."

🌸 Khairun Nisaa (rahimahallah) not only ensured that she awoke for Tahajjud every day, she made an effort, every day, to wake up even earlier. This is the true spirit of a believer – he always strives to improve and better himself in Deen and acquiring the proximity of Allah Ta'ala.

🌸 For a person to exert himself in 'ibaadah for a few days is easy. The true test of dedication is where a person remains committed all the time, and it is this dedication that draws the special love and mercy of Allah Ta'ala. Khairun Nisaa (rahimahallah) was so dedicated to her Tahajjud that let alone foregoing it due to ill health, she was not even prepared to awaken a little later and decrease the time for her Tahajjud!

An Upbringing of Piety

The greatest accomplishment of Khairun Nisaa (rahimahallah) and the highlight of her life was perhaps the exemplary manner in which she raised and moulded her son, Moulana Sayyid Abul Hasan 'Ali Nadwi (rahimahullah). Moulana (rahimahullah) was orphaned at the tender age of nine. It was thus his mother who single-handedly attended to his upbringing.

Khairun Nisaa (rahimahallah) was extremely kind and compassionate towards her son, especially since he had lost his father. However, there were two aspects regarding which she was unrelenting and extremely strict.

The first was salaah. In this regard, she would not tolerate even the slightest negligence or laziness. If her son ever fell asleep without performing his 'Esha Salaah, she would wake him up and make him perform it, even if he was in a very deep sleep. Similarly, she would wake him up at the time of Fajr Salaah and send him to the masjid. Thereafter, when he would return after salaah, she would make him sit and recite the Quraan Majeed.

The second aspect regarding which she was very strict and firm was his behaviour with the servants and the poor. If he ever ill-treated a servant or their child, or displayed arrogance and treated them rudely, she would force him to ask them for forgiveness and beg their pardon.

Moulana (rahimahullah) explained the great impact that this had on him throughout his life in the following words, "This (approach, which my mother adopted,) benefited me greatly in my life and instilled within me the intolerance for pride, arrogance and oppression. It also impressed upon me the seriousness of the sin of looking down at people and treating them badly. Furthermore, due to this, it was always easy for me to acknowledge my mistakes (throughout my life)."

When Moulana (rahimahullah) went to Lucknow to study, his mother continued to monitor his progress and check on him through his step-brother. She also continued to write letters to him, advising him and giving him guidance in various areas of his life.

Lessons:

❋   Although it outwardly seems as though she was only strict regarding two aspects, the reality is that she actually impressed to her son the importance of the entire Deen. The reason is that Deen is primarily divided into the duties of Allah Ta'ala and the duties of the creation. By being strict on salaah, she instilled the importance of the first category of duties in his heart, and by being strict on his behaviour with the servants and the poor, she instilled the importance of the second category in his heart.

❋   Even after Moulana (rahimahullah) grew older and left home to pursue his Deeni studies, his mother remained concerned over his progress and continued to check on him and advise him. This is because the parents' concern for their child is until they die. Hence, parents must never stop making du'aa for their children, and so long as they are able to, they must continue to advise them and encourage them towards righteousness.

Dedicating her Son for Deen

The dream of Khairun Nisaa (rahimahallah) was for her son to develop within himself the Deeni qualities for which their family was renowned, and for him to become the flag bearer and true representative of his pious predecessors and his father. The dream to see him carry the name of Islam throughout the world was indeed her greatest dream and aspiration, and it was for this that she constantly engaged in du'aa.

The decision to make him an 'Aalim was an extremely difficult one, since the importance of English, secular education was on the rise and was being promoted very strongly in their family. Her nephews and other relatives were studying abroad, in London, America, Germany and Japan. Hence, the family members were exerting immense pressure and insisting that Moulana (rahimahullah) should not become an 'Aalim. However, she did not buckle under this pressure and insisted on him pursuing his Deeni career. Her passion for this can be gauged from the following excerpt of a letter that she wrote to him:

"From your family, all have acquired secular education and they will continue to do so. However, there is nobody who is acquiring the knowledge of Deen. This is the need of the time. Despite not possessing any English education, how did those pious elders (of the family) attain such a position? 'Ali! If I had a hundred children, I would ensure that I give Deeni education to all of them. At present, you are my only child (who can study Deen). May Allah Ta'ala allow me to see the fruit of my sincerity by allowing you to do the good work of a hundred children. May Allah Ta'ala allow me to be successful and honoured in both worlds and may He allow me to be regarded as a mother of many children, aameen!"

Lessons:

❁ We do not advocate that a child be deprived of secular education. However, we advocate and insist that a Muslim child should never be deprived of Deeni education, as without the basic knowledge of Deen, how can he fulfil the obligations that he owes to Allah Ta'ala, and how can he correctly fulfil the rights of people? If we neglect to give our children a proper secular education, then at the worst, they will be called 'unqualified'. Even then, this will not impact on their material progress, as many 'unqualified' people are millionaires today. However, if we neglect to give them a proper Deeni education, we will be handicapping them in their journey to Jannah, and for this, we will be held accountable before Allah Ta'ala.

❧ Khairun Nisaa (rahimhallah) had seen that most of her family members had devoted themselves to secular studies, however none of them were becoming 'Ulama and hoped to serve Deen. She thus dedicated her son to the Deen of Allah Ta'ala, understanding that this was the best career decision that he could ever make, as this career would earn him more 'profit' than any other enterprise.

An Envious End

During the last few years of her life, Khairun Nisaa (rahimahallah) had become almost totally helpless. She could barely see as her eyes could not perceive more than light and vague shadows. Her mind, however, was still perfectly functional. Her legs had become extremely weak, to the extent that she could only move about while leaning on someone for support.

Despite her weakness, frailness and her advanced age of over ninety years, she still remained committed and punctual on her zikr, recitation of the Quraan Majeed and other nafl 'ibaadah. The women, children and other members of the family would constantly visit her and spend time with her in order to benefit from her goodness and blessings.

Once, towards the very end of her life, she became very sick, causing everyone to become worried and anxious. However, with the grace of Allah Ta'ala, she finally opened her eyes and regained her senses. It was at this time that Moulana (rahimahullah) was requested to travel to Bhopal to render some service of Deen. However, due to his mother's condition, he was in a state of hesitancy, unable to decide whether he should go or stay.

In this state of indecision, he mentioned to her that he had been requested to travel to Bhopal. He also mentioned to her, "Mother! I completely submit myself to you! If you are even slightly unhappy, I will not travel. There are still two days remaining (until the journey), whatever you command me to do, I will fulfil." Khairun Nisaa (rahimahallah) replied, "'Ali! I will never hold you back from fulfilling the work of Deen. Go! Allah is the protector and helper."

A few days after Moulana's (rahimahullah) departure, when she had awoken for Tahajjud Salaah and was being led to the bathroom, she fell, breaking her shoulder and wrist due to the darkness and her sleepiness. On account of her injuries, she was in extreme pain. Message of her fall was sent to Moulana (rahimahullah), and as soon as he learnt of it, he returned.

In this state, where her pain and discomfort was increasing and her injured bone was hurting severely, she ensured that she performed all her salaah and completed all her zikr and tasbeeh. Furthermore, she did not utter even a single word that was directly or even indirectly a complaint or an expression of impatience.

The pain which she was undergoing was such that it would have caused even a young, strong man to scream, yet at 93 years of age, when she was weak and frail; she was an embodiment of patience and gratitude and thus did not allow her tongue to utter anything besides the zikr of Allah Ta'ala. At the most, when the pain was once very intense, she said, "O Allah! Forgive our sins!"

On the last day of her life, when the time of Chaasht Salaah (Salaatud Dhuha) set in, then without saying anything to anyone, she began to search for the soil, which was normally kept at her head side, so that she could perform tayammum. Seeing that she intended to make tayammum, somebody mentioned to her, "The time of Zuhr has not yet set in." Hearing this, she remained silent and did not say anything. However, she kept feeling around her with her hand, searching for the soil. The soil was thus given to her and she performed a complete tayammum. She had, by this time, become slightly unresponsive and there were lapses in her concentration. Nevertheless, she performed two rakaats of Chaasht Salaah, after which her awareness further decreased.

When the time of Zuhr set in and the soil of tayammum was brought to her, she performed a complete tayammum and then performed all four rakaats of her Zuhr Salaah. Observing the scene, all the family members marvelled and wondered at how she miraculously regained her concentration and attention when it was time for salaah.

Although she was again unresponsive, strangely enough, she was feeling about with her right hand, as if she was searching for something. The family then realized that she was searching for her tasbeeh, as her tasbeeh would always remain in her hand.

After she fell and was injured, her family had taken the tasbeeh out of her hand as they feared that moving the beads of the tasbeeh would aggravate her injury and cause her pain. However, the habit of making zikr on the tasbeeh was so deeply ingrained in her that her hand automatically searched for the tasbeeh, and in its absence, her fingers formed a circle and rubbed against each other as they continuously moved, as if she was counting on the actual beads of a tasbeeh.

At 3pm, her condition changed and she broke her silence. Now, with every breath that she took, she began to make zikr aloud. Hearing her making zikr aloud in this manner, her family gathered around her. Her zikr of 'Allah! Allah!' was so loud and clear that it could even be heard from outside the house. She continued making zikr for approximately three hours and forty-five minutes, and her family members present had never before witnessed a scene of such tranquillity. It seemed as if the mercy of Allah Ta'ala was raining down.

During her final moments, various people recited Surah Yaseen softly. They did not feel the need to make talqeen (recite the kalimah aloud as a means of prompting and encouraging the dying person to recite it) as she was already engaged in the remembrance of Allah Ta'ala.

At quarter to six, her zikr abruptly ceased and the environment was enveloped by silence. After a few seconds passed, they realized that her soul had left her body.

In this manner, Khairun Nisaa (rahimahallah), who had spent her entire life exerting herself in the worship and zikr of Allah Ta'ala, had now departed to her Rabb, and her lifelong restlessness and concern of passing away on imaan was comforted.

Lessons:

❀ Even though she was injured, in pain and very advanced in age, Khairun Nisaa (rahimahallah) remained punctual on her salaah and 'ibaadah. On the other hand, we often shirk in our obligations based on the smallest excuse. On account of this commitment, 'ibaadah had become her second nature.

❀ Khairun Nisaa (rahimahallah) lived a life of obedience and loyalty to Allah Ta'ala, hence she was blessed with a most envious death. She passed away most peacefully, with the name of Allah Ta'ala on her lips. If we wish such a death, we will have to lead our lives like her. If we live with Allah Ta'ala's name on our lips, insha-Allah we will die with His name on our lips.

Index

A

Aaishah, 62
Asmaa, 101, 117
Assisting Others, 108, 130, 161, 162, 169, 173, 177

C

Caring for Elderly, 223, 224
Charity, 46, 49, 71, 73, 78, 107, 108, 155, 157, 170, 175, 177
Chastity, 9, 10, 33
Children, 27, 30, 32, 40, 43, 44, 123, 157, 207, 208, 209, 210, 211, 212, 215, 222, 224, 226, 242, 245
Choosing the Right Spouse, 100, 144, 151, 231
Company, 155, 208, 210
Compassion, 108
Competing in Good, 28, 120, 122, 125, 126
Correcting One's Wrongs, 69, 82

D

Divine Assistance, 8, 37, 38, 52
Du'aa, 7, 9, 17, 20, 23, 25, 26, 31, 32, 137, 148, 239, 241

E

Entertaining Guests, 201, 203, 236, 237

F

Faatimah, 131
Faith in Allah Ta'ala, 52, 77, 78
Family Ties, 94, 102, 155
Fear of Allah Ta'ala, 82, 142, 144, 185
Forgiving Others, 76, 77, 95
Friends, 153, 154

G

Generosity, 73, 78, 79, 170, 175, 177, 199, 202
Gratitude, 153, 154, 189

H

Haajar, 11
Halaal Consumption, 41, 44, 183, 184
Halaal Earning, 144, 159, 160, 183
Hayaa, 34, 36, 38, 58, 61, 66, 85, 86, 104, 105, 115, 131, 132
Hifz, 227
Hijaab, 58, 60, 61, 65, 66, 83, 85, 86, 92, 105
Hind, 109
Humility, 86, 87, 88

I

Ibaadah, 29, 30, 33, 34, 149, 197, 198, 238, 240
In Laws, 200, 203, 205, 234

J

Jealousy, 47, 49

K

Khadeejah, 58
Khairun Nisaa, 222

L

Love for Rasulullah (sallallahu 'alaihi wasallam), 96, 109, 112
Love for Sahaabah, 146, 147
Loyalty, 14, 15, 18, 19, 135, 192
Loyalty to Allah Ta'ala, 8, 9, 41

M

Maimoonah, 60
Maryam, 24
Modesty, 34, 36, 38, 58, 61, 66, 85, 86, 104, 105, 115, 131, 132

N

Niqaab, 58, 65, 66, 83, 92, 105

O

Obedience to Allah Ta'ala, 90, 102, 144
Obedience to Husband, 135, 150, 151, 199, 200
Obedience to Rasulullah (sallallahu 'alaihi wasallam), 68, 100, 115

P

Patience, 16, 18, 19, 136, 247
Pleased with the Decree of Allah Ta'ala, 11, 27, 35, 36
Pleasing Allah Ta'ala, 19
Pleasing the Husband, 52, 154, 199, 200, 202, 203, 236
Preference to Others, 84, 85, 237
Priorities, 90, 151, 198
Purdah, 58, 60, 65, 66, 83, 85, 86, 92, 105

R

Remorse, 81, 163, 165
Respect, 91, 92, 178, 179, 180

S

Saarah, 7
Sabr, 16, 18, 19, 136, 247
Sacrificing for Deen, 130, 196, 217, 218, 245, 246
Sadaqah, 46, 49, 71, 73, 78, 107, 108, 155, 157, 170, 175, 177
Safiyyah, 89
Salaah, 7, 9, 33, 145, 148, 150, 153, 154, 197, 242, 248
Serving Others, 205, 236
Serving the Husband, 15, 106, 154, 236
Shukr, 153, 154, 189
Simplicity, 73, 74, 200, 201
Steadfastness, 41, 244
Submission, 11, 12, 67, 68, 96, 114, 115, 238

T

Ta'leem, 209, 211, 239
Tahajjud Salaah, 186, 223, 240
Taqwa, 142, 144
Tawakkul, 11, 13, 53, 191
Trust in Allah Ta'ala, 11, 13, 35, 53, 78, 191

U

Ummu Khallaad, 104
Ummu Salamah, 60
Ummul Baneen, 152

V

Verifying Information, 49, 77, 93, 94

Z

Zainab, 106
Zeal for Knowledge, 197, 198, 208, 210, 218, 238
Zubaidah, 166

www.ingramcontent.com/pod-product-compliance
Lightning Source LLC
LaVergne TN
LVHW012037070526
838202LV00056B/5521